# Personal, Professional, and Positive
# The 30-Day Challenge

*by*

Danyelle Little
Telie Woods

Copyright © 2015 by Danyelle Little and Telie Woods

All rights reserved.

This book or any portion thereof may not be reproduced or used in any manner whatsoever without the express written permission of the publisher except for the use of brief quotations in a book review.

Printed in the United States of America

First Printing, 2015

ISBN: 978-0-9971514-0-4

Contents

## I. Personal

Reinventing You ........................................................... 1

It's a Love Thing .......................................................... 5

Bad Habits Gone Good ............................................. 10

Operation Cleanse and Purge ................................... 13

Attitudes are Everything ............................................ 16

Keep Calm and Sleep Deep ...................................... 20

Write Your Heart Out ................................................ 23

Make More Memories .............................................. 26

Digital Detoxification ................................................. 30

Grow your Gifts ......................................................... 33

## II. Professional

Manage Your 24 Like a Pro ....................................... 37

Your Professional Mission Statement ...................... 41

Embrace Your Company's Culture .......................... 44

The Art of Over-Performing ..................................... 48

On the Job Workout Plan ......................................... 51

Multiple Money Streams ........................................... 55

A Wake-up Call to Excellence ............................... 62

The Incredible Power of Concentration ................ 65

Iron Sharpens Iron (Masterminds) ....................... 68

## III. Positive

Random Acts of Kindness ...................................... 72

Lend a Listening Ear .............................................. 76

The Power of Words .............................................. 80

Living the Positive Thought Life ........................... 84

An Environment of Encouragement ...................... 88

Order is Everything ............................................... 92

Defeat Won't Define Your Destiny ......................... 95

Patience is Worth the Wait .................................... 98

Standing Strong in Storms .................................. 102

Shine Like Nobody's Watching ............................ 106

# Foreword

There's a subtle difference between self-improvement and self-reinvention. Although both concepts are directed towards the ratification of one's current state, self-reinvention takes more of a drastic approach, where one invents again, anew. Enter *Personal, Professional, and Positive*, a disquisition that acts as a 30-day roadmap to self-reinvention. The co-authors act as knowledgeable tour guides navigating you through the vast jungle of mediocrity, to the final destination of a re-invented "You"!

The three-pronged approach taken by the authors is strategic, providing us with targeted directives to improving your current state. During my preparation for the writing of this foreword, I began to digest the contents, especially the "Challenges" and "Life Hacks," and can say assuredly that habits formed as a result of this reading will lead to many successes in your life.

So get ready to embark on a powerful journey. Approach the contents herein with an open mind. Make a deliberate effort to ingest the precepts outlined in *Personal, Professional and Positive*. Set high expectations, take notes, and prepare to be challenged. Anticipate noticeable improvements in everything from your attitude to how you manage your time. Take stock of where you are before reading this book, then again upon your completion. Give yourself a hearty "congratulations" for the self-reinvention that will have definitely taken place. Cheers to your imminent success!

Maurice White

Co-Founder, Think Positive Magazine

# Introduction

Have you lived up to the person you always knew you could be? Could one of the reasons be that you aren't regularly challenging yourself to greater heights personally and professionally?

These are the two hard questions we've personally asked ourselves for years. It wasn't until we got real about our struggles that we were able to snap out of the matrix of mediocrity. Seriously confronting the demands of your day, in a successful way, takes a positive attitude. That's why this book is for everyone. No matter your social or professional status, infusing positivity in our personal and professional lives is a must.

We wrote this for the go-getter and ultimate person of action who wants to live their best life. This guide will help create a truly meaningful personal eco-system and eliminate obstructions from your path to greatness. We are excited to present both a male and female perspective of self-love, professional prowess and mindfulness. Let's be honest, many of us have drifted away from virtuosity in our lives and the excellence on the job. Many of us can stand a refreshing mentally, not to mention an overhaul of our attitudes.

Once we discovered the power behind positive thinking and its connection to daily habits, productivity began to skyrocket. Creating positive habits and destroying negative ones became a lifestyle. Habits will make or break you. This epiphany provided the passion to publish this guide.

If you are anything like us you want to see others win. We believe everyone can become the best in whatever it is that they love. We're all about changing for the betterment of a greater future financially, mentally, physically and spiritually. Are you? If so, keep reading.

*Personal, Professional, and Positive*

We know that you will find this book essential yet practical, compelling and timely. Take a moment to delve into each chapter and challenge, as a way to start your mornings. Utilize a quiet space to soak in the material and for best results, read daily.

We thank you for reading *Personal, Professional, and Positive: The 30-Day Challenge.*

# I. Personal

One

# Reinventing You

***Challenge:*** *Make the decision to embrace personal enhancement, take the necessary time to plan your reinvention, and set a realistic identity goal to create a new normal.*

THERE IS A PORTION OF the population that feels great about their current lifestyle. Then there are those of us who feel dissatisfied with where we are. These people are desperate for a change personally or professionally, and sometimes both. The usualness of our daily routines can grow mundane pretty quickly. If you were to take an internal audit of your personal life, would you discover things about yourself that need an upgrade? The awesome thing about life is that it's never too late to begin investing in yourself. Our willingness to change is crucial in any quest to achieve greatness. Life isn't about finding yourself; it's about creating yourself.

Consider the amazing transformational life cycle of the butterfly. After an incubational period a crawling caterpillar emerges from a cocoon with a different design, but also, more importantly, a different purpose. It can now pollinate, mate, and migrate. In its caterpillar state, it only munched on leaves all day. When reinventing yourself, you play the role of a potter as well as the clay. As our world makes its daily turn we mold the clay of our lives, tweaking things, fixing the broken, mending the torn around us. It's when we begin to fix things that winding roads begin to straighten. Hurdles in the road begin to smooth out.

## Reinventing You

As we make adjustments in and around us, we begin to awaken potential. Life-changing potential can't afford to lie dormant within us. When we operate in excellence, someone else does too. Which is why we should always look for a place of true significance in our communities and ultimate distinction at our jobs. Becoming a standout gives you an advantage over those unwilling to bend. You never want to suppress potential with a stubbornness to change. Progression means acquiring new traits and skills. A few small changes can yield big results, and often the prize can be greater than the price.

Here are a few ways to refresh ourselves and create instant access to the extraordinary:

Switch your style; your approach to fashion states who you are without you having to say a word. If you've been wearing the same old slacks, skirts, or boring shirts, then it may be time to shake things up. Look through a fashion magazine for inspiration, or ask a clothing-store employee for a little guidance. Pick up a few signature pieces. For men who need a little help with their wardrobe, consider enrolling in a clothing subscription service. You'll receive monthly shipments of casual and business swagger upgrades. Sites like trunkclub.com will even include access to a personal stylist from the company. Dress for where you want to go, not where you've already been.

Remodeling your look should not stop at your wardrobe. Go outside of your culinary comfort zone and try new foods. There is more to life than burgers and fries. Experience some delicious French delicacies, African entrees, or spicy Indian dishes. Dare I say revisit some of the foods you didn't like as a child? You may find that your tastes have changed over the years.

Maybe you've always wanted to learn a new language. Why not learn Spanish so you can use it while on vacation in Spain, or when you're

*Personal, Professional, and Positive*

applying for a particular job? Invest in some language software and start studying. Whatever language you choose, you're sure to learn a valuable dialect you can use for the rest of your life.

Reinvent your relationship with spontaneity. Spontaneity can put you in a realm of living versus existing. Phenomenal things happen when we ride the wave of life. No longer do we wish for the weekend, or yearn for special events. Embrace the unplanned and the random passionately. Chances are good that there are some exhilarating activities you've always wanted to try. From skydiving to whitewater rafting, there are many ways to become a thrill seeker. You probably talk about all the traveling you're going to do someday. Why not take an exotic trip on the fly? Book the tickets and make the reservations. When you are relaxing on a beach in Hawaii, or strolling down the streets of Italy, you'll be glad you did.

It takes time to reinvent yourself. It's a journey we all need to take several times, at different stages of life. If you continue to educate yourself, you'll always keep an open mind. It's the best way to run this race we call life. I like to look at life like the controls on a radio.

Press:
*Play* for laughter; life is always better when you're laughing.
*Pause* for the memories; take a second to reflect on past.
*Stop* the pain; right any wrongs.
*Rewind* the happiness; revisit your place of pleasure.

You can't get your childhood back, but you can recreate it! Take a childhood memory and bring it back to life. You don't have to wait for Saturday mornings anymore; you can pull up your favorite childhood cartoon on YouTube and pour a big bowl of cereal. If it is baking cookies with your mom, pay her a visit with cookie dough in hand. If it's a great photo with your siblings, why not recreate the same picture today as adults. Things like these refresh relationships with the people that enjoy some of the same memories.

> **☞ Personal Hack**
> Find a mentor. Someone who has systematically self-evolved. If you have trouble finding a direct mentor, allow books to mentor you indirectly through their authors.

This chapter kicks off the book because excellence is about always being prepared to bring your A+ game when opportunities present themselves. It's about being on point at all times and never allowing your skillset to get outdated. There are two main comfort traps many of us struggle to shake off.

1. We hold on to things we should be letting go of.
2. We don't take the necessary risks that are often prerequisites for success.

You sometimes have to make daring decisions to fulfill your dreams. You are far too intelligent to be the only thing standing in your way. Right now is the oldest you've ever been, and the youngest you'll ever be. Don't hesitate to make smart alterations to the elements that make up your life. A new you may be exactly what you need. Greet a new season or even each new day with a new, reinvented you.

> *Life is what happens to you while*
> *you're busy making other plans.*
> – Allen Saunders

Two

# It's a Love Thing

***CHALLENGE:*** *As your next gift in celebrating loved ones, instead of purchasing a gift, create one from the heart. Write a letter to them expressing how much they mean to you, or take a photo of the two of you and get it framed in order to show your appreciation.*

---

AS BUSY INDIVIDUALS, WE SPEND so much time working on our careers that it begins to take over our lives. It is time that we remember whom and what we are working for. Our loved ones should be at the core of our lives, and the main reason why we work so hard for what we have. It is time that we get back to basics and center our heart on those we love the most, and not have our total focus centered on our work and other distractions.

Taking time out to commune with your loved ones and foster relationships is also an added stress buster, because it can give you pause to focus on something else for a change. I know when I get some time in with the special people in my circle, I walk away full, and feeling so much better than before. The busyness of life takes its toll—but the time I put in with my people refuels me when I am running on empty.

A few years ago when I was caught up in growing my business and the day-to-day operations of running my own endeavor, I lost sight of the importance of friendship and putting time in. I rarely took any time out to spend with those closest to me, and it began to show. I didn't know how to relax, and I was both anxious and stressed out all of the time. It was as if I closed myself off to those who loved me the most—not on purpose, but because I was operating with an "island" mindset, one where I alienated people to focus on my tasks at hand. I forgot that while growing my business, I needed to also nurture my personal side and the relationships I had developed. It couldn't all just be work and business, or I would risk running myself into the ground. I now understand and appreciate friendships and close bonds. Having an outlet where I could share my life with others while running my business made a happier and healthier me. And I could also get support from them when needed, which is key to any professional who is looking to empire-build.

With any relationship, guidelines are a must. In order to help keep those most important to us thriving and nurtured, spending time with one another is critical. Many relationships that are splintered and don't have a solid foundation are often filled with chaos and negativity, which in turn breeds drama and misunderstandings. When a relationship is planted firmly in love, it flourishes and triumphs no matter what obstacles may come its way. In order for it to be a real, tight-knit affair, there have to be rules in place so that love, communication, and growth can be fostered abundantly.

Below are a few examples of relationship rules that I follow that help keep me and the people closest to me connected and of one accord. They also assist me in being a good friend to others:

*Personal, Professional, and Positive*

**Talk it out to clear up any misunderstandings: don't assume.**
Discussions can get heated; words can be taken the wrong way, and cause unnecessary friction. In order to counter discourse that may arise in a disagreement or misunderstanding, it must be discussed and hashed out—even when it is uncomfortable to do so. Don't allow negative feelings to build and fester. This will splinter your connection and bond. Talk it out, be respectful of one another, and be reasonable. Try to listen more than you talk so that you can truly understand the other person. Work out the issues in a calm manner. Jumping to conclusions and assumption can be a catalyst for arguments. Instead, ask questions, clarify, and get to the heart of the matter.

**Think first before you speak.**
Is what I am about to say helpful or harmful? Am I being kind or responding defensively to be mean or spiteful?

**Share helpful thoughts and encouragement with one another daily.**
It doesn't matter if you are tired, or if one of your favorite television shows is on. Take time out of each day to share a kind and loving word with your loved ones. It can be a quick text or email letting them know that you are thinking about them, or a note in their lunchbox or briefcase with a word or two of encouragement. When you share these types of thoughts on a regular basis, you create momentum within your tribe that cannot be blocked. You and those closest to you are building muscle, which can then be used to combat any trials that may come your way.

**Be a branch for extended family or those who don't have close familial ties**

In an age where our families may live in other cities, states, and even other countries, it is essential that we also reach out to extended family members not near us. Make it a family habit to reach out to other members whom you may not see as often. Utilize social media to update and share photos and important events. You can even create a Facebook group for your family and use it as the connection spot for everyone. Don't forget your elders; make sure to check up on the older generations in the family as well and do your best to see them as often as you can. And if you have friends or loved ones that are estranged from their families or aren't very close, make sure to let them know you are there for them as well so they don't have to be alone.

> ☞ **Personal Hack**
> Create a monthly calendar by using Google Calendar, or a free online template. Each month, update it with important dates for the family, close friends, or loved ones. Make sure to schedule activities or get-togethers.

Your relationship rules should be utilized often, and everyone should be held accountable to them, because they promote habits that are integral in long-lasting relationships. The more that you practice them, the more they become a daily part of your lives.

You can also indulge in doing activities with friends and loved ones regularly, and take turns deciding what the activity will be. Once or twice a year, a group of my girlfriends get together in another city and we have

*Personal, Professional, and Positive*

a Girls' Weekend. We've rented a cabin in the woods, had sleepovers in hotel suites, and have had a road trip or two together, all of which have brought us closer together. It doesn't matter how much time has passed between events—we all fall back into our roles and always have memorable experiences that we will can look back on. If money is tight, it can be something as simple as a family game night of Monopoly, Taboo, Connect Four, or even cards. Or pop some popcorn, put in a DVD, and have some fun together. It's all about quality, not quantity.

When you create a life that is focused and centered on your loved ones, it improves the way of life for all of you. As long as you all are being the best you can be as a unit and love one another unconditionally, it can make everything else in your world better.

*Friends are the siblings God never gave us.*

*– Mencius*

Three

# Bad Habits Gone Good

***Challenge:*** *Break a bad habit today. Identify it. Confront it. Replace it with a good habit.*

---

FAST FOOD, SMOKING, AND REALITY television may not be vices of yours, but I'm willing to bet you have a bad habit you've wanted to break. Left uncontrolled, these habits grow and develop into addictions. Bad habits are like a nice comfy bed: easy to get into hard to get out of. It seems as though many individuals go around the same mountain again and again. Before you know it, years have gone by and you're still dealing with the same thing. It's hard to explain why we keep making the same mistakes. We could take the easy, though not incorrect, way out and blame imperfection. We all have faults and flaws. The good news is that a lot of our blemishes are fixable.

How do you break the power of that bad habit? There must be a decision made, one serious decision toward positive change. This is necessary to begin analyzing exactly what kind of affect it's having on your life. Self-correction is about using your thought life as a catalyst to make better decisions in familiar circumstances. You were meant to grow mentally, spiritually, physically, and emotionally. The key is putting something productive in its place, and allowing its influence over you to weaken over time.

We must aggressively seize control of the things in our lives. This will cut off the power of whatever is hindering you from moving forward. I

*Personal, Professional, and Positive*

know it's easier read than done, but you can do it. This chapter doesn't call for perfection, but rather the inner instinct to win in life. There is an internal war within each one of us, and the side you feed the most will win every time. If you continue to give in to a desire that will not, and has not, benefited your life, then you halt your forward progress. If you halt forward progress, growth stops.

We get older with every day, but getting better has to be the daily goal. Meeting the demands of this goal requires a plan. You can't defeat a powerful foe without a strategy. Your bad habits do their job of distracting you with a ton of consistency. Is there something that you are doing or thinking that is creating drama that you don't need right now? After years of waging war with myself I found there are a combination of things I could do to correct myself when I'm out of line. Break out the pen and paper, and list any detrimental patterns you've noticed.

Here are 5 steps I take to turn bad habits into good ones:

1. Identify the habit; expose it as an adversary.
2. Discern it; write down why you think it became a craving.
3. Break the cycle; go on a cold-turkey fast of the fixation.
4. Make a public pledge (if it isn't a serious habit); tell a friend.
5. Replace with an alternative habit valuable to your life.

> ☞ **Personal Hack**
> Research the Habit Loop. It consists of three elements: a cue, a routine, and a reward. Grasping the concept of these elements can aid in understanding how to change bad habits and form good ones.

## Operation Cleanse and Purge

fulfillment. What I found was that my life was impeded with negative thoughts, things, and relationships that were clouding my vision of the future. I found that while my personal and professional categories were filled to the brim, my future category was not. It was then that I got the hint: if it isn't something assigned to my future, it can't play a role in my current personal or professional life.

Are there people you frequently come in contact with that cause chaos in your life? When it's obvious a person brings bad times along, it's time to detach. Sometimes we must go as far as cutting them off cold turkey. You must realize that not everyone qualifies to be in your circle. We must begin to sanitize our social relationships. These are people who need to be purged from your life, or, at the very least, kept at bay and only dealt with when necessary. There is a lot of power in loving someone from afar. I will pray for you. I will be there if you really need me but I need to keep you at a distance. It's sad, but sometimes a necessity to keep your sanity without destroying a relationship. By ridding yourself of such debris, you are purging your personal environment of thoughts and things that don't lend themselves to a healthy lifestyle.

You can then move onward to things in your home life. Take a Saturday afternoon and clean your refrigerator or stove inside out. Get rid of the unhealthy foods and beverages that can lead to weight gain, high blood pressure, and other harmful conditions. Reset your system with healthy raw foods, organic fruits, and vitamins. Get into the habit of reading labels for harmful additives that we need to stay away from. Our bodies need also need a cleanse and purge on a regular basis. I recommend that you perform a thorough cleanse at least every three months to expel toxins that can lie dormant in your body's organs.

> **☞ Personal Hack**
> Add an alert on your phone or tablet once a month to remind you to remove unnecessary items from your life and environment.

What we take in visually can also be mind-waste. Pornography, violence, and other images that we see or listen to also need to be exiled. Not only do these things keep our minds "busy" with unhealthy distractions, but they can also cause habits that hurt others and ourselves. Clear your computer of this type of debris; throw away magazines and other things that can cause unhealthy thoughts and behaviors, which are unhealthy and harmful. You also must purify your thoughts. Rid anything from your mind that brings you down or makes you unhappy. Focus on things that bring you joy and make you smile.

Sometimes you have to actually restore peace. Peace in your mind, your home, your heart. This process is important for moving forward toward a more optimistic and happier lifestyle. Making these changes can lighten your load and open possibilities that may have proved to be difficult before.

*Don't let negative and toxic people rent space in your head.*

*Raise the rent and kick them out.*

*– Robert Tew*

Five

# Attitudes are Everything

**Challenge:** *Make amends with anyone whom you may have drifted apart from.*

---

AN ATTITUDE IS LIKE A pair of sunglasses: it changes the way we view and respond to things. Few things are more telling about who you are than our outlook on life. Our viewpoint of people, situations, and circumstances will seemingly express the true condition of the heart. Whether good or bad, right or wrong, every one of us can stand an attitude adjustment. Our perspective on life can always benefit from believing the best about ourselves and others.

Although our attitudes are a way of feeling or thinking, they can manifest themselves physically through the body's behavior. It's called body "language" for a reason—it speaks! Have you ever asked a waitress for a clean fork and you got a little bit of attitude along with your new fork? Notice that without her even speaking, you can tell she is either having a bad day or doesn't want to be there at all. We've all been there before, but some of us can become a prisoner to our emotions. What is your attitude when things are going well? Our immediate responses can be a natural defense mechanism against drama. That's a good thing if, and only if, they are wise responses.

Let's look at a couple of attitudes that affect our responses:

*Personal, Professional, and Positive*

1. Humility vs. Pride

Humility says we are no better than others. It takes humility to recognize that we need people, and even on our best days we're severely flawed. It takes humility to initiate peace when others want to war with you. This attitude of the heart leaves no room for judgment, vanity, or arrogance. It endorses taking the proverbial back seat. Even when we win, if we are meek in spirit, honor and grace will arrive to accompany your successes. We should never let our victories go to our heads. Exalting ourselves is completely unattractive, so let's leave it up to others if they see fit. A wise person actively humbles himself—before his circumstances do.

Pride is a trick to get us to think about ourselves instead of the needs of others. It can fool us into thinking we can operate independently of people we actually need. Pride won't let you submit your will to the will of another. It won't let you learn from life's lessons. It won't allow you to leap to the service of others.

2. Gratitude vs. Complaining

Gratitude is the attitude that attracts wonderful opportunities and relationships. It's a magnet for the miraculous. Gratefulness will draw happiness closer every day with the rising of the sun. It's one of the best ways to start your days. As a matter of fact, let's take a look at today. You woke up with the activity of your limbs, breath in your lungs, blood in your veins, and in your right frame of mind. You made it through last month, last week, and last night. Don't take these blessings for granted. Begin to verbally acknowledge these things, and silently appreciate the small things. The secret to having it all is believing you already do.

Complaining is an outward expression of negativity that attracts new negativity. Will your disapproval of a circumstance change it? If change won't come, it is simply a waste of breath to complain. Our dissatisfaction with things we feel should be different isn't wrong, but your declaration of it is. No matter how bad things can get, your life is still someone else's Disneyland. Being overcritical, whining, and making excuses have zero benefit to your life, and this behavior taints the lives of others. No one wants to be associated with this kind of person. If you find yourself complaining, stop yourself. Begin to articulate phrases of faith, gratitude, and contentment.

### 3. Forgiveness vs. Grudges

Forgiveness is an attitude of grace that is meant to extend mercy to an offender. More importantly, it is a mindset that liberates you from the eight-hundred-pound gorilla of blame on your back. You earn esteem by overlooking the wrongs of others. Sometimes we hang insignificant debts over the heads of those we've helped. That's unacceptable. Showing a high level of compassion toward someone who owes you stores up mercy for the very day you need to be pardoned. You reap what you sow, so correct your mistakes with people. You've hurt people before, and you've been hurt. If you've offended someone, you have the power to frustrate them—but you also have the power to set them at ease. This is why it is equally important to extend that mercy when a person offends us with their words or actions. Taking the higher road is always recommended.

Grudges can turn into its older cousin—hate. Do you remember that time five years ago when you were extremely upset? Does it really matter now? One of the best things we can do is immediately forgive when someone has wronged us. The worst thing you can do is allow offenses to remain unchecked. If unregulated, offenses grow roots like a tree: deep into the soil of your heart, becoming increasingly hard to uproot.

*Personal, Professional, and Positive*

> ☞ **Personal Hack**
> Research and try the EFT (Emotional Freedom Technique)—it will help you change your attitude in a flash. This technique uses the energetic meridians of your body to help release bad energy and begin feeling better in just a couple minutes.

Look at your heart like a garden. Dress it, cultivate it, and keep weeds out. Let's all make the decision to adopt attitudes of love, joy, peace, patience, and faith. Love has a glowing effect on all of us, and is virtually the answer to all of life's ills. Joy uplifts when worlds around us crumble. Peace brings unity to a global community. Patience is the fruit of a good attitude while you're waiting for something. Faith refuses to consider circumstances and speak of future events as if they've already happened.

Goodness, kindness, and temperance are all virtuous attitudes we must return to. There is absolutely no way to sidestep when people or situations offend us. Since this is impossible to avoid, the question then becomes this: how will you respond when they happen? Your responses most certainly determine your future. If you can take a positive approach to life and refuse to waver a good demeanor, opportunities will abound. Attitudes are contagious. Is yours worth catching?

*Attitude is a little thing that makes a big difference.*

*– Winston Churchill*

Six

# Keep Calm and Sleep Deep

**Challenge:** *Completely shut down all technology at least one hour before bedtime to turn your mind off and prepare for rest.*

---

IT'S A KNOWN FACT THAT most Americans do not get enough sleep. Most of us are overworked, over-stressed, and over-stimulated, which can cut into our sleeping time. Many experts recommend seven to eight hours of sleep a night, but according to Web MD, less than half of adult Americans do not get that much sleep.

A lack of sleep can cause major problems, including fatigue, weight gain, and a lower immunity. We've all been taught to grind, hustle, and work toward a better life, which often includes working well into the night. This is okay to do every once in a while, but over time, it can cause issues like those described above.

A more positive and healthy lifestyle needs to begin with a full night's sleep—regularly. We must get more rest to be able to conquer what challenges face us on a day-to-day basis. A well-rested mind can do things that one low on rest can't do. You will perform better, be healthier, and be able to achieve more. By getting a full night's sleep, we are doing our body good. In turn, this can help us do good for others.

According to WebMD, an extra hour of sleep can really come in handy. It can cause a better sex life, less pain, improved health, less stress, better weight control, and clearer thinking. With those benefits, why would anyone question getting more sleep?

*Personal, Professional, and Positive*

When I get on a regular schedule of going to bed at a decent hour each night, it shows. I am well rested and able to tackle my day. As an entrepreneur, I tend to want to work into the wee hours of the morning, but I understand that in order for me to be an ultimate success, I have to put my best foot forward. So making a habit of going to sleep at a decent hour every night bodes well for my overall health, well-being, and prosperity.

> **☞ Personal Hack**
> Apply a drop or two of lavender diffused or essential oil to your pillow and/or sheets. This is a calming scent that is recommended to prepare your body for sleep.

Most of us don't get enough sleep because technology keeps us plugged in. Is it hard for you to "turn off" at night? You can follow these tips to make it easier for you to get into a "sleepy mood":

- Turn off the television and stop watching it at least 1.5 hours before your planned bedtime. If you can, nix the television in the bedroom. This can lead to more rest and relaxation, which your body needs.
- Leave your laptop, tablet, and other devices in the other room, or turn them off completely.
- Use an activity tracker to track your sleep patterns. This can help you see where you may have trouble sleeping.
- Don't drink anything with caffeine after 7:00 p.m. This can help you sleep better.
- Use lavender essential oils or melatonin to help you go to sleep if you have trouble sleeping.

When you are in Stages 3 and 4 of sleeping, tissue growth and repair

## Keep Calm and Sleep Deep

happens. Your energy is rebuilt, and you experience muscle development. After that, REM sleep occurs, which provides energy to the body and the brain. This also helps improve daytime performance, reflex time, and agility.

In addition, sleep experts also recommend taking short naps during the day if you are tired or are lacking rest. When working in an office, this may prove difficult to do, but you can always try to find a quiet area on your lunchtime to take a quick nap. It is recommended that the naps do not go over 20-30 minutes, as you may throw off your sleep later on that night.

Think of sleeping as your restoration period. It helps bring your body back to its center so you can be refreshed and replenished for the next day. Not getting enough sleep means your body isn't able to restore itself as it should. It's like your computer or smartphone—if you don't reset or turn it off regularly, it begins to glitch. Your body is definitely not a machine, but after so much time of not being shut down, it too will begin to show symptoms that it needs a refresh. Don't wait until those symptoms begin to make themselves apparent. Refresh yourself fully each and every day.

If you've tried all of the above and you still have trouble sleeping, consult your physician, who can help you get to the root of the problem.

*A good laugh and a long sleep are the best cures in the doctor's book.*

*– Irish proverb*

Seven

# Write Your Heart Out

***Challenge:*** *Purchase a journal to express feelings you can't verbalize. Over time, see how these thoughts manifest in your actions and behavior.*

There is something very cathartic and therapeutic about putting your feelings on paper. It can be an outlet to express yourself, let go of anger, and other things that may be holding you hostage. Writing can give you the release that you need in order to move forward.

Journaling is an exercise that allows you to write down your thoughts and put them to paper. I have been journaling for over fifteen years now, and doing so has allowed me to unload things that I may not have been able to otherwise. Once these feelings are released, they make way for new ones to enter.

Holding on to baggage like frustration, anger, and resentment can cause stress and other factors that aren't healthy for you. Why keep negative feelings inside, when you have a way to give them up and turn them loose?

When you journal, you can release these feelings, and, in doing so, see areas where you may need to reevaluate yourself and improve. It can be a positive way to vent, share, and release. And it also can be a learning tool that causes you to look at your decision-making and thought patterns. It can be very useful for personal development.

Writing down your feelings doesn't always have to be a negative release. It can also be an expression of positive feelings, too. I love sitting down with a cup of hot tea on a Sunday morning and writing about my week. I don't have time to journal every day, but Sunday mornings are my chance to recap. I share my life, recent travels, events, accomplishments, and goals. And if I have any negative feelings, I share those, too. When I finish writing, I feel light and free.

Since I have been journaling for so many years, I've acquired over fifty different notebooks. I often refer back to them, reading over memories, and they always bring me back to that time. I can look back and reminisce on those days, and also see my progression. I can see how my writing has changed, and how I was before I changed my outlook. It is almost like having your own time capsule.

> **☞ Personal Hack**
> Use the Day One app to help you journal on your phone, tablet, or computer.

Journaling is not a replacement for prayer and meditation. It is just another place where you can share your thoughts without judgment. If you don't have anyone to confide in or talk to, writing down your thoughts and putting them to paper can be the next-best thing.

If you haven't written in a journal before, I can tell you that doing so can change a lot about the way you think. It can also be a personal case study as you grow and evolve. Sometimes, when we see our thoughts written out in black and white right in front of us, it gives us a different perspective. It can cause us to reevaluate, and perhaps make better choices and wiser decisions.

*Personal, Professional, and Positive*

You can start a journal by writing in a notepad, notebook, or diary. If that isn't your thing, you can even type out your journal on your computer, or use a blog—which is, in fact, an online journal—and fill it with your thoughts and feelings. You can keep the online journal private if you don't want to share it with anyone, or write anonymously.

If none of those ideas above strike your fancy, you can use an audio journal. Use your smartphone and download an application that allows you to record audio. Then, during a quiet moment, talk into the application and create your audio journal. Listening to them and playing them back can give you the same directives as reading your written words.

Our words have power, and so do our thoughts. As these thoughts build within us, we need a healthy way to unload them. Your journal will never judge you or make you feel inept. Using it can help you grow, release, and make necessary changes.

*Writing is an exploration. You start from nothing and learn as you go.*

*– E.L. Doctorow*

# Eight

# Make More Memories

***Challenge:*** *Create a budget, then open a separate account strictly for family/friend fun.*

---

THERE IS A TREND IN American homes that is quickly becoming the norm. People are working more and playing less. We are functioning more mechanically in a culture that has high demands and seeks quick results.

Outside of work, our social lives have gone digital. Our faces are constantly buried in our smartphones. Dating has moved to the Internet, and we even rely on Facebook to tell us when it's a friend's birthday. Does eight hours of work, five hours of television and laptop screens, with six hours of sleep sound familiar? This schedule doesn't leave much time for living. The same technology that is empowering us is also dehumanizing us. All of the great technical advancements of the human race push us forward. However, the more we integrate technologies in our lives, the less human interactions we have. We must make time to take our lives back. Once we stop rushing through life, we'll be amazed at how much more life we have time for. When it's all said and done, our memories are the only thing we will have left. Not your possessions, and certainly not your money.

Do you find yourself shooting down your friend's ideas of going skiing or taking a road trip? What about when your spouse recommends a family vacation or a weekend getaway? If so, pay attention to the reason why you

## Personal, Professional, and Positive

decline and the frequency with which you do so. You may notice the years are flying by, disregarding any plans we may or may not have established. Life is much more than co-existing and working to pay our bills.

The truth is, you aren't much more than an account number to utility companies and lenders. I'm not saying don't pay your bills, but let's be clear—these companies are benefiting from the fruits of your labor more than you are! We have to change the way we think. We should be quick to create memories so that during bad times we can enjoy flashbacks of the good times. When loved ones leave us, our brain's files should be filled with wonderful reflections of silly and serious moments. These are the moments our lives are made of.

Begin to use a portion of your money exclusively for entertainment purposes. No matter your tax bracket, this can easily be accomplished. You will carve out time for the things you value. The question is, what do you value the most? If you value friends and family, systematically deduct a slice of your twenty-four hours for these relationships. The health of our associations require time, attention, and, oftentimes, money. Not all of your time, but some time. Not all of your money, but some money. Make it a point to gather your loved ones, especially if you don't have a specific reason. It always feels good for everyone after a chance to reminisce about the good old days. Reconnect. If you can make this lifestyle change, you most likely won't have regrets later in life.

Not only are we working our fingers to the bone, but our children are almost as busy as we are. We all want our children to be as grounded and well rounded as possible. We sign them up for whatever activity their heart desire. The little ones are only young once. They will be adults for much longer than they will be kids. Choose to spend time, not just money, on them. Don't forget that our pets are family and love a little quality time as well. Take Fido to the lake, or start including him on your daily run.

> **☞ Personal Hack**
> Interview older family members with your smartphone's camcorder about their youth and past lives. Compile the videos into one video for the whole family to enjoy.

Out of everyone, the people we probably need to spend extra time with is our parents. Make it a point to spend more quality time with them. We are so busy growing up that we forget they are growing old. I challenge you to dedicate a day each month to taking Mom to dinner or treating Dad to a round of golf. Schedule some random family cookouts with your siblings. Like most relationships that begin early in life, our connection with our brothers and sisters can grow stale if it isn't kept fresh by reliving childish banter.

We certainly can't forget the family we get to choose: our best friends. Entertain friends at your home once in a while. It's time to get back to the lost art of the house party. Revive the "get-together." What better way to be with those you want to catch up with? You get to play the music you used to love, show off those bartending skills, and display the food you've been waiting to brag about. Eat and chill with some positive people.

It seems like women get the idea, as they vacation much more often than men. Fellas, it's okay to get the band back together and take an international trip. But until the trip happens, get the guys together for a game of hoops. When is the last time you guys went bowling or shot pool? If finance-guru Suze Orman says you are approved and the wife allows, go

*Personal, Professional, and Positive*

ahead and build that man cave. The good times are sure to roll.

From birthdays to holidays, sporting events to music concerts, there is always an excuse to get together. Making more memories enables us to look back on life with a smile. Bursting out with laughter at distant memories is precious. Living your life with no regrets is priceless. Let us refocus on the things that really matter in life. Happiness is simple—don't complicate life. If you love someone, tell them. If you miss someone, call them. If you want to meet up, invite them. Moments come to an end, but memories last forever.

*Sometimes you will never know the value*

*of a moment until it becomes a memory.*

*– Dr. Suess*

Nine

# Digital Detoxification

***Challenge:*** *What does a detox look like for you? Create and facilitate your own digital detoxification fast for a full week.*

---

TECHNOLOGY, GADGETRY, THE TWENTY-FOUR-HOUR NEWS cycle, and social media have most of us tuned and plugged in to the world all day, every day. As soon as something happens, within minutes we all are sharing, retweeting, and updating our statuses with thoughts and opinions. There is nothing wrong with this as long as it is done in moderation. But problems may arise when we overuse technology: it can become an issue that will manifest itself negatively in our lives.

As someone who has built a business online, I understand the extent to which the Internet and the devices that bring it to us have shaped my life. I am a huge proponent of a healthy digital lifestyle—one that uses technology for good. Sharing positive messages, connecting with others, and enjoying healthy entertainment are elements of a healthy Digital Lifestyle. When technology becomes a habit that is hard to tear away from, or begins to impede your life personally and professionally, then it is time to take a step back and reevaluate.

Participating in a Digital Detoxification regularly as a part of your lifestyle is a wonderful way to disconnect from the World Wide Web and get in tune with the real one. Allowing yourself to detach from the matrix gives you the opportunity to have in-person contact and connections, while doing other things that don't require being turned on and plugged in. It's healthy, and very necessary, to unplug.

*Personal, Professional, and Positive*

We all experience precious times and moments. How many times have you noticed a couple dining together but barely talking, glued to their phones the whole night? Or the person in the car next to us who is texting and driving, almost running another driver off the road? What's more important than driving safely so you won't put others and yourself in danger?

Banning the Internet from your life for a temporary period of time is a great way to spend time with people that matter to you. Afterward, you can come back restored, refocused, and renewed.

> ☞ **Personal Hack**
> Purchase a disposable camera during your digital detox and use it to take photos. Get the photos developed as a memory of your time spent unplugged.

You can totally attack your detoxification any way you see fit. I advise that you do a detox from social media at least once or twice a month. I usually do this on the weekends when I am busy doing other things. Doing it regularly helps get you in the habit. It may seem a little weird at the beginning, but I promise you that after a few times, it won't be so foreign to you. You will even begin to enjoy the time "away."

With your Internet-free time, you can use it spending Tech-free time with your family, catching up with old friends, spending time in meditation and prayer, or reading a book and getting some much needed rest. Do you have a project or business idea that you keep putting off because you don't have enough time? When you are fasting from the Internet and social media, you can use it to build your empire. Things that you have been putting on the back burner can now be in the forefront in your world.

You can also perform a detox from gadgets and electronics. Make it a

## Digital Detoxification

point to shut down your phone—or at least put it away—during dates and nights on the town with your mate. Or you can do something like the Five Minute Rule, where the two of you check your phones for five minutes, and when time is up, away the smartphones and tablets go.

I've participated in such group dinners where we all stack our devices on the table so we are fully engaged in the conversation, listening, and making eye contact. The first one who reaches for their phone has to pay for dinner, and since you don't want to be that guy or girl, this gives you an incentive to log off and enjoy yourself.

I also have a No Tech Zone policy in my bedroom. My laptop isn't to be used in my bedroom, and I actually keep it in my laptop bag in my office. I only bring it in my bedroom during special circumstances like a business emergency that has to be addressed immediately. My phone, after 10:00 p.m., goes into Do Not Disturb mode and only notifies me if I receive a call or text from VIPs. That way, I am able to get rest and truly unplug and relax.

I recently stopped reading books on my iPad before bed, which is how I went to sleep every night. Now I buy actual books to read. This keeps me from checking social media sites and emails after hours. I am enjoying the books better because I'm not being interrupted by notifications.

The awesome thing about your Digital Detoxification is that you can design and personalize it your way—just make sure to have a plan in place, and make it a part of your life on a consistent basis.

*The more ways we have to connect,*

*the more many of us seem desperate to unplug.*

*– Pico Iyler*

Chapter 10

# Grow your Gifts

***Challenge:*** *Take a free strengths-assessment test online to help discover your gifts, strengths, or character potential.*

---

CAN YOU IMAGINE GIVING YOUR kid a gift and your child not taking the time to unwrap, open, and enjoy it? This is essentially what happens if we don't take the time to explore and activate our God-given gifts. Gifts, not to be confused with talents, are often irrevocable. They are divine, eternal, and cannot be taken from you. It is imperative that you identify your gifts.

Talents are more of a natural skill and are temporary. For example, if a person has an innate ability to play the piano, it can be taken away due to serious injury. Talents are inherited from forefathers, and are naturally present since the moment of birth. Talents can include public speaking, teaching, singing, accounting, writing, painting, and cooking.

Gifts, on the other hand, are more spiritual in nature and can include encouragement, generosity, and hospitality.

Discovering a gift does not happen overnight, but it can be a direct link to our particular purpose in life. So be on the lookout for cues when others express things like "wow, you're really good at that," or "I can't believe how well you handled this." If you are gifted at serving people, you may want to join a local community service organization, like Habitat for Humanity or a local food bank. Do you typically show an uncommon amount of mercy toward others? Volunteer at a homeless shelter or your community's church. Are you a bigger giver than anyone you know? See, it is the nudging of these gifts that gives us hints that they exist. They are a clue to your calling. It's the very things that have you feeling incredibly compassionate.

> ☞ **Personal Hack**
> Once you've uncovered what your gift is, you must take time to develop and grow it. Literally begin setting aside time specifically to operate in it.

The abilities we've been endowed with are typically not meant for us, but for the edification of others. It's why you think and act the way you do. There are people that cross our paths that need the positive energy of qualities built into our personalities. We are each like refrigerators filled with fresh food. To keep the produce within us from spoiling, we must plug into a power source. It's never too late to "plug in," preserving our gifts for others to feed off of.

Let's take the gift of wisdom, for example. With wisdom you have an uncommon understanding of what to do when faced with difficult decisions.

You may even have the ability of discernment. This gift enables the accurate ability to tell where someone is earnest or has an agenda. It is a distinguishing of whether or not to do things in particular.

Faith is also a gift. Those with this gift see life quite differently. They tend to have an amazing amount of confidence in all situations, and they do not fear bad news.

We must pay very close attention to identify our children's gifts as

*Personal, Professional, and Positive*

well. It's our job to assist in the development of undiscovered powers and abilities. Put them in the best position to harness potential—shape them to make a difference and to be productive members of society.

Few people ever uncover the significance of gifts and reap the rewards. Be open to learning more about yourself. Your gift tells you what to do, your passion shows you where to do it, and your personality tells you how. Let's acknowledge our abilities and be grateful to the source of them. We are individual and unique, yet we must work together and remain dependent on each other to complete life's puzzles. The things you are passionate about are not random: they are your calling.

*The meaning of life is to discover your gift.*

*The purpose of life is to give it away.*

*– Pablo Picasso*

# II. Professional

Eleven

# Manage Your 24 Like a Pro

***Challenge:*** *Examine your to-do list and move the most difficult task into the top. Knocking that one out reduces the chance of procrastination.*

---

TODAY IS A GIFT, AND it's time we begin treating it as such. We arise with renewed hope for the things we need and desire. What does a successful day look like to you? Have you ever wondered why some people are more successful than others? The answer may lie in your daily routine. Successful people are married to their calendar and manage it with precision. This is a concept easily understood but difficult to master. In the twenty-four hours that it takes for planet Earth to rotate on its axis, you can knock out everything on your plate.

In a perfect world, you would get your recommended eight hours of sleep, wake up rejuvenated, spend time in prayer, and go for a run, all before the rest of the house wakes up. This is very possible. Maybe you should consider joining the 5:00 a.m. club. The 5:00 a.m. club is an exclusive group of people able to muster enough discipline to prepare for slumber so that they are able to wake up at dawn. Can you imagine the amount of productivity you'll possess?

This club is exclusive because many of us go to sleep late, wake up late, rush to work, and use artificial "pick-me-ups" to replace natural energy throughout the day. Trade in that cup of coffee or 5-hour Energy for lukewarm water immediately after you wake. Some Asian cultures practice this to jumpstart the organs, renew cells, and even cure illness. If you don't have your physical energy in good shape, then your mental, emotional, and spiritual energy will all be negatively affected. Make the necessary changes to your routine to be a better steward of your body.

Prepare like a professional. We have to begin to look at each day as a doorway. The door to success swings on the strength of two hinges: opportunity and preparedness. When you miss an opportunity, it's gone. That specific chance now belongs to the past. New opportunities do arise, however, and the best way to seize them is to be as prepared as possible when things present themselves.

Always remember these 5 Ps: Proper Preparation Prevents Poor Performance.

For instance, the person that performs best in a job interview has studied the job description, researched the interviewer, and updated themselves on the company's history and current industry trends. This is the person that walks away victorious. We can have the same victory over the challenges of our daily lives. Good planning and insight allow you to lie down without fear of what tomorrow may bring. When we begin to attack the tasks of the following day before it even arrives, you hit the ground running once it shows up. This is why athletes go through extensive training before their season starts, and endure practices before game time.

It's the things you do over and over again that shape your future. Staying focused in the present moment is a great way to help us use our time more effectively. If you are going to win today, make sure your activities are prioritized.

> **☞ Professional Hack**
> Start each workday by making a list of tasks with the heading "Get it done today."

Prioritize like a pro. Do you prepare to seize the day ahead of time, or do you casually waltz in and out of your days? How we prioritize the things we plan to happen, as well as the unforeseen, will determine if you've mastered your day or if your day has mastered you. Make it a point to arrange your responsibilities in order of importance. If you have five things to do, only two are really important. You can leverage time by giving less attention to activities that are urgent but unimportant, and devote more time to those things that are important but not necessarily urgent. There isn't much you can't get done when you prioritize tasks and handle the unexpected with finesse.

I've learned to prioritize my duties of the day in a way that is easy to follow. Each of my activities are regulated into categories tagged with traffic-light colors.

*Green-time* activities take high priority, push toward your goals, and make you money.

*Yellow-time* activities need to be completed yet slow you down if done out of order.

*Red-time* activities steal time from your day and should be dealt with outside of business hours.

Our daily grinds can have a tendency to wear us down. We have so much information coming at us that quiet is a rarity. The classic professional is caught up in a whirlwind of messages to process and act upon, including home and the workplace. We should make it mandatory

## Manage Your 24 Like a Pro

to sit still for a period of time each day. Silence is golden. Silence gives the brain a much-needed break from the race it runs. It can be a form of self-healing, which is what happens when we sleep. But stillness can heal us while we are awake. We need to proactively take a moment to maintain good mental health and happiness. Find a half hour in your day where you retreat from everything and everyone. No food. No music. Just pure solitude. Create an atmosphere of calmness for yourself. This gives our souls an opportunity to revitalize.

In America, aka "the no-vacation nation," when we go on vacation, we don't actually relax. Go on a retreat with a loved one and really unwind. Find a sanctuary; build one if you have to. Go for a walk. Meditate. Take a nap. Read a book. Take a shower. Spend time in prayer and quietly wait for an answer. These are all ways to restore when your routine won't let you relax. Sometimes the therapy of silence is all you need to hear. Peace of mind during the grind is the goal.

We have a choice every day to act on yesterday's good intentions, or to get an early start on tomorrow's regrets. Even though you cannot go back and make a brand-new start, you can start from now and make a brand new ending. Tomorrow, let go of everything you didn't do right today. Each day means a new twenty-four hours, and everything's possible again. Don't count the days: make the days count!

*Tomorrow is the first blank page of a 365-page book. Write a good one.*

*– Brad Paisley*

Twelve

# Your Professional Mission Statement

**Challenge:** *Create a 30-second mission statement for your professional career and follow it daily for career success.*

---

WE'VE ALL READ MISSION STATEMENTS, and perhaps have even created them, for brands and corporations. These mission statements lay out the purpose of the company and how it will serve its customer base. These days, it is virtually impossible to launch a business without this very important key ingredient.

For professionals, it is vital that we also have a mission statement for our careers and how we conduct ourselves accordingly. Creating and following your objective of how you will operate on a daily basis can help fuel you even more, and give you a calculated mindset to adhere to. This can also offer more consistency. When operating from the basis of your core professional values, you can better serve yourself and the company that you work for.

We've all asked ourselves this question: what is my purpose? In your career, your purpose should be one that is mutually beneficial for you and your employer. With your professional mission statement, you boldly set the tone for what your purpose and value is to the workplace, and this helps you solidify your strategy for the future. While other coworkers are going about their day-to-day without this key ingredient, you are able to conquer your objectives clearly and with precision.

## Your Professional Mission Statement

To create your professional mission statement, you must participate in self-reflection. Who are you when it comes to your career? What do you offer and provide? Are you a problem solver, and if so, how do you go about solving problems? What are your core values, and how do they play into your professional role? Once you begin to answer these questions, you can move toward crafting your statement.

Here's an example of a professional mission statement from an account executive at a leading investment firm:

*To work diligently in problem solving, negotiating, and helping others see the big picture as they save for retirement in an honest fashion that will lead the customer to prosperity, wealth, financial freedom, and financial health.*

This statement is powerful and effective. It speaks to his goals, his mindset, and even his work ethic. It expresses the core value of honesty, and mentions how he wants to actually work with his clients. He also lists his strengths of problem solving and negotiating, which showcase his skillset. He has outlined a motto that will serve him well in his career. His statement isn't employer specific, but rather profession specific. He can take this proclamation to any company in the financial industry and it would work.

Also in his statement, you can see his passion for the business. It is a motivating affirmation that can help not only guide him daily as he performs his job duties, but inspire him as well. Seeing this mission statement regularly can improve his productivity and sales.

Your mission statement should do the same. It shouldn't be a bloated list of your gold-star moments. It assists you in excelling and becoming a top talent in your office. A well-written professional mission statement is like having a theme song. Just as a boxer comes out to the ring to a song that pumps him up and prepares him for the fight of his life, your mission

*Personal, Professional, and Positive*

statement should also work as a theme song for your current and future goals.

> ☞ **Professional Hack**
> Stuck on creating a mission statement? Ask colleagues and friends to describe you in your personal life, and then professionally. Keep a running tally of responses and use this to craft your mission statement.

The declaration that you draft may take you a while to complete. But once done, it can help give you an edge over the other employees in your company that do not have one in place, making you in the top talent pool of your organization. Once your mission statement is crafted and complete, make sure to post it in your office or cubicle so that you can refer to it daily. Tape it to your monitor, or print it out and put it in a frame within view. Visually seeing your statement consistently will begin to synergize it with your workflow and give you much-needed encouragement.

A mission statement helps make you accountable to your purpose. When we are operating in our purpose, we are living the best lives we can in both the personal and professional spectrum. I don't know about you, but I like having my own set of principles that help guide me within my career. It's these principles that help set us up for something greater and more meaningful. Make sure that you do not skip this important and pertinent step.

*All you have to do is write one true sentence.*

*Write the truest sentence that you know.*

*– Ernest Hemingway*

Thirteen

# Embrace Your Company's Culture

***Challenge:*** *Lead your coworkers and colleagues by implementing professional strategies that support your company's culture.*

As we discussed in the previous chapter, most major companies have a mission statement to support the goals and vision they have in place. These goals and the way they are utilized throughout becomes the company's culture.

Company culture is the behaviors, experiences, attitude, and leadership methods that foster the "mood" of the environment that you work in. The very feel of the workplace, from the psychological impact to productivity and performance, all stem from the corporate culture set forth. When you understand the inner workings of whom you work for and how it manifests into a productive and fruitful work environment, then you are better able to run with the ball toward the goal line of success. You can be a steward of leadership and knowledge, which can put you in the driver's seat, allowing you to move up the ranks.

You must remember this: management only wants to have the best represent their company, and they often seek out leaders. I bet that if you are reading this, you are probably a leader and have an ambition that is strong and unyielding. You've been assigned by your destiny, not only to shine bright for yourself, but for others as well, so you have work to do.

*Personal, Professional, and Positive*

Understanding, implementing, and fostering the workplace mainline can set you apart from the rest.

Why, you may ask? Here's the kicker: most people who work for your company do their job rather well. But they don't totally know or understand the essence of the very company they work for. They are clueless when it comes to truly understanding what makes the business tick, which can be an asset for you. Because you will learn it, study it, and make it a part of your work ethic while on the job, thus proving yourself formidable against any competition.

> **☞ Professional Hack**
> Memorize your company's mission statement and utilize key messages from it in meetings, company emails, etc. Use this to create a leadership team amongst your coworkers.

Whether your office is a shiny, bright place with mostly happy people or a dark dungeon with endless file cabinets and cubicles, the company culture affects everyone in the organization. But the company culture is as only as strong as the sum of its parts—the employees. So your leadership becomes truly valuable when you can create a shift that is beneficial not only to the employees, but to the company as well. Creating that shift can offer you opportunities that you never thought were possible for you.

You were hired because of your experience, your work ethic, and your letters of recommendation. But you will move up in the company and position at a higher level with the work that you do after you've been hired. It doesn't matter if someone else has more seniority that you, or has more degrees than you—once you are in that door and do your job, you can go above and beyond and lead while initiating the culture of your workplace. That is where the magic happens—for you and the company.

## Embrace Your Company's Culture

How can you get to know and understand your company's culture? Here are a few suggestions for you:

1. Start with HR.

Upon being hired at the company you now work for, you probably met with someone from Human Resources who went through the employee handbook with you. In this handbook is usually a copy of the company's mission statement, and other vital information about it that most people overlook. Use that handbook to get to know your company culture backwards and forwards. Doing so will give you a better understanding of who you work for, which can only bode well for you.

2. Know your company's origin and history.

Understanding how your company began and its rise to prominence not only helps you know the history of your workplace, but can also be an asset during presentations, meetings, etc. The history and the origin of the business is a foundation of its culture.

3. Know the Movers and the Shakers.

Understanding the environment in which you work also means knowing the key players. Who's the CEO, COO, and CFO? How long have they been with the company, and what moves have they made? The company culture is often reflected in the rank and file of upper management, so understanding how they tick can help you plot your course to success.

4. Study the environment.

Is your office a quiet and hushed place, or is it vibrant and casual? Do you often have team-building activities and projects, or is it a more on-your-own kind of vibe? Knowing the environment that you work in can

*Personal, Professional, and Positive*

help you not only do your job better, but also be able to lead others and help them as well.

Understanding your company's culture can give you a totally different perspective, setting you up for the bigger picture. You have the opportunity to change your life as well as others around you, giving you the chance to move up the company ladder faster than you anticipated.

*No company, small or large, can win over the long run without energized employees who believe in the mission and understand how to achieve it.*

*– Jack Welch, former CEO of GE*

Fourteen

# The Art of Over-Performing

***Challenge:*** *Ask your employer what his biggest issue is, solve it, and present the results.*

---

GOING TO THE NEXT LEVEL in life means exceeding expectations. Simple satisfaction of basic requirements just won't do any longer. This professional key unlocks excellence in social and work relations. Pushing yourself to perform past your current abilities is much easier said than done. Initially, it takes an active, consistent mind renewal. You'd have to change the way you look at your career, friends, or spouse. Going the extra mile means exactly that. It's the difference between ordinary and extraordinary.

When the crowd stops and when others relax is when you break through the invisible wall of mediocrity. Getting obsessed with greatness means staying hungry for the next level. Why should we think like this? Simply because those around us need more examples of what passion looks like. Your level of pursuit will spark a flame in someone else, ultimately causing a domino effect of excellence. A just-enough attitude will produce just enough. Just enough money, just enough recognition, and just enough respect.

That is fine, but this book is written for those looking for a higher level. If there is one thing you can bet on, it is that people that live in a "just enough" world, despite over-performers, are usually clueless as to why someone would do more than what is expected. If you are willing to set aside pride and any false sense of entitlement, then you are going expose yourself to grandiose possibilities. You are the perfect person to set the standard with coworkers and leadership alike.

Loyalty and kindness equals a good reputation among those in authority over you. As companies grow, leaders move up the corporate ladder. These people have to be replaced with future talent and hopefully they're blessed enough to be at an organization that promotes from within. Even if your efforts aren't spoken of, someone is watching. Hard work and respect are virtues that rarely go unnoticed. If your efforts appear before blind eyes, you must keep yourself encouraged. This is where self-motivation creeps in and pushes you into overdrive. Begin to take instruction like a military cadet. Take on the tasks that other associates won't do. Going the extra mile whispers your name in the ears of people that can promote you.

I'd be lying if I told you companies care; they don't. At the end of the day, the numbers are all that matter. They care about performance, and the sooner you understand how they think, the sooner you can free yourself to capitalize and not be a victim.

> **Professional Hack**
> Give your brain and body a break. Take a vacation to refresh inspiration and you'll be on a motivational high once you return.

Many employers subscribe to the notion that all employees are expendable. However, you become irreplaceable with high-quality work, a competitive spirit, and a pleasant attitude.

## The Art of Over-Performing

In addition, here are a couple traits that over-performers have embedded deep within their professional DNA:

Respond more quickly: your ability to be prompt will show that you value the relationship.

Keep promises: your integrity will take you places. Say what you mean and mean what you say.

Raise your IQ (intelligence quotient): your wisdom will grant you distinction if you don't allow it to grow stale. Seek information, take classes, and join groups to build upon what you know.

Raise your EQ (emotional quotient): your soft skills make the connection to the world around you. Focus your attention to relationship building and become a pro at conflict resolution.

After you've adopted a new viewpoint, opportunities to excel past the norm will expose themselves. Look for them. Once you spot them, take control but refuse to get overwhelmed. You are more than your job, and the last thing you need is your home life affected negatively due to burnout. The easiest way to manage this is to under-promise and over-deliver.

Everyone has their season, and I believe this one is yours. Your dream doesn't have an expiration date. Take a deep breath. If you keep your focus on the process of overachieving and not the results, you will win every time.

*Go the extra mile, because doing your best in this moment*

*puts you in the best place for the next moment.*

*– Oprah Winfrey*

Fifteen

# On the Job Workout Plan

***Challenge:*** *Commit yourself to being more active during working hours for a healthier you.*

---

IF YOU ARE A PROFESSIONAL, then chances are you are spending many hours of the day at your desk. Minutes can turn into hours as you go through your daily tasks and to-dos, and before you know it, you've spent half the day sitting in one place. Many careers call for a sedentary lifestyle, especially when working in an office. While it is important for you to do your job well, you probably aren't getting as much activity during the workday, which isn't healthy.

Our work environments can lead us to eating lunches and snacks at our desk, which is unhealthy-habit-forming. Add artificial pick-me-ups with caffeine-riddled coffee and soda-machine blues, and it becomes a cycle that continues to repeat itself. Before we know it, we've begun packing on the pounds, and our blood pressure and cholesterol begin to be affected.

There are no benefits to gaining weight, eating in an unhealthy manner, and not getting much activity during the eight-plus hours spent at work. That road only leads to more problems and health risks, and you don't have time for that. So you've got to consider options that can help you avoid salty snacks, high-fructose beverages, lunch on the run, and things that offer you a quick jolt.

## On the Job Workout Plan

Start thinking about your health while at work. In the span of your hectic workday, you can also get some activity in and make better decisions when it comes to what you are putting in your body. You probably plan meals for your family that are healthy and nutritious. And you may even pack lunches for your children that are doctor approved. But what about also dedicating some planning time for your workday where your health is concerned?

There are plenty of things you can do to be healthier at work, and the benefits are numerous. Alongside more stamina and a clearer mind, the quality of your projects will improve, which can lead to promotions and higher salary. Forget about gaining weight—if you make it a point to be more active while on the job, you might even lose a pound or two. You will look better, be able to handle tasks more vigorously, and gain more confidence, which is a huge asset professionally and personally.

> **☞ Professional Hack**
> Acquire a workplace buddy and encourage them to get active throughout the day. Work as accountability partners to help motivate one another.

With just a few changes, you can totally transform your mind, body, and soul while at work. And these actions can fit well within your workday while you are working hard.

Stand during phone calls. If you are on the phone quite a bit during your day, you can get out of your seat and get moving. While on your call, simply stand up, and if you are up for it, you can also walk in place. Doing so will get your heart rate up and burn calories. This doesn't have

*Personal, Professional, and Positive*

to be vigorous, and you can stop at any time. It sure beats sitting still at your desk.

Walk to colleague's office instead of sending an email. During any given day, you probably send a countless amount of emails to coworkers. Instead of doing this, when you are able, simply walk to their office or cubicle and communicate in person. Take a notepad with you and write down the details of your discussion, and when finished, you can summarize the conversation in an email once you are back at your desk.

Take the stairs whenever possible.

If you work on the thirtieth floor, then taking the stairs may not be an option for you. But if you work in a smaller building, or just need to go up a couple of floors to another department, then why not take the stairs? It gets you active, out of your chair, and will help you get fit.

Keep healthy snacks at your desk.

Vending and soda machines at work mean one thing—stress eating. Combat this by keeping an arsenal of healthy snacks at your desk. Trail mix, granola bars, wheat crackers, fruits, and veggies are all examples of quick snacks that you can bring to work with you. You can also try smart foods like peanuts, which are a good source of B vitamins and protein that also fight brain fatigue. Peanuts are also free of cholesterol and provide long-lasting energy that can take you through the day. Just make sure to opt for unsalted or low-sodium peanuts.

Opt out of takeout.

There are very few takeout restaurants that offer healthy food. So while everyone else is passing around menus, know that you are staying on track because you brought your own lunch. Take that leftover chicken breast you made for dinner and chop it up for a salad with spinach greens.

## On the Job Workout Plan

Or opt for a turkey wheat wrap and a bag of no-bake chips, which is filling and better for your waistline.

Do you need some motivation to help cheer you on to stay active while in the workplace? Monitoring your movement is easy these days with the help of activity trackers like a Fitbit or a Jawbone UP band. In addition, most smartphones have an app that can track your steps, heart rate, caloric intake, and more. Use these tools to your advantage, and reap the benefits of a more active work life.

It has been said that your body is your temple. What we put into it and how we treat it are important, no matter where we are. You spend most of your days working, so while you are doing so, you have to keep your body and its health in mind. Choosing to be more active at work can not only bode well for you in the workplace, but also create lasting habits that you can share with others. With the benefits of a sharper mind and a body that participate in movement regularly, it can be just what you need to get an edge over your competition.

*Take care of your body. It's the only place you have to live.*

*– Jim Rohn*

Sixteen

# Multiple Money Streams

***Challenge:*** *Add a stream of income by freelancing your skillset. Take your specific talent and lend it to the public for a fee.*

---

AN ASTOUNDING 76% OF AMERICANS live paycheck to paycheck. If your primary income stream dried up for whatever reason, how would you continue to support your lifestyle? If you take a serious look, it's actually very risky to have only one main source of income. I used to manage a sales team for an insurance company, and short-term disability insurance was always an easy sell because no one had an answer to the question "If you lost the ability to earn, due to an injury or illness, how would you keep the lights on?" What if your spouse loses the ability to earn? If your household income was only functioning at 50%, how long would you be able to survive? These are the hard questions we often fail to ask ourselves.

One of the most impactful books I've read in recent years changed the way I look at revenue streams. Multiple Streams of Income by Robert Allen was an eye opener. It sparked my mind about how and when to add revenue flows. With the cost of living rising higher, it's harder to raise families on modest money. It's almost necessary to have multiple streams of income to have a chance at thriving in our current economy.

There are three major categories of income: active, passive, and portfolio income. Active income is your job or career. Passive income streams are generated on a regular bases without much maintenance once you set them in pace. Portfolio income comes from investments, interest, royalties and capital gains. I love passive cash-generating opportunities because they continue to pay you, month after month and year after year. No matter if you are looking to add $100 or $1000 to your monthly income, begin eyeing income opportunities that are recurring at a low risk.

> **Professional Hack**
> Seek out a social lending network where you can lend your money to other people. You act as the bank. You can invest money in lending online, where investors can earn up to 13% annualized returns.

If you are a bit savvier but just haven't pulled the trigger on an investment, real estate is a good place to start. Owning a rental property can become a source of passive income, creating wealth for years to come. If you're social, start an investment club with a tight circle of friends. Grab a book, study the club logistics, wrangle about six best friends and collectively begin planting financial seeds sure to produce a garden of gains.

A part time job is also good idea nowadays. Many people see little choice but to swallow pride, buckle down, and create another income stream. Be as resourceful as possible. Consider a flexible situation, like using your vehicle as an Uber driver on weekends for extra income. If you're feeling really entrepreneurial, then it may be time to start a business your community can use. If you already own a company, you can still create an additional source of income from your already existing source. For example, if you are a blogger, why not expand your brand with fashionable gear your audience will buy? Leveraging an existing brand can be a seamless way to generate added income.

Friends, there is a prerequisite to satisfy before multiplying streams.

## Personal, Professional, and Positive

You must remember the golden rule of establishing an emergency account first. Having a liquid account for when "life happens" is the basics before you begin investing. This may seem elementary, but you'd be surprised by how many people don't have a dedicated emergency reserve. The rule of thumb is save three to six months' worth of expenses. Assuming you are beyond the basics, multiple streams of income can supercharge your efforts in creating a retirement plan.

Whether your goal is to retire comfortably on an island with your spouse, or if you just want to live off a hefty nest egg, it's smart to proactively make moves in the realm of retirement. At the top of the year, I interviewed Alexandria Cummings, president of Mind over Matter Financial, on my Think Positive podcast. Mrs. Cummings had this to say when asked about the near future for young professionals: "We won't have the benefits of retirement our parents had. You have to become your own retirement plan. You have to become your pension." This is why taking your financial future into your own hands is paramount.

If you don't build an entrance for money to flow through, how will you receive it? No longer can we expect our jobs to fund our dreams. Multiple, strong, dependable flows of income will prepare you for wealth. Creating wealth isn't a mystery: it's a formula. The only reason a person isn't creating wealth is because they either don't know the formula or are not implementing it. Your current cash flow should create additional cash flow. We must get to a place in our finances where we are acquiring assets that earn more money. Acquire assets that produce cash flow and invest the profits back into more assets that produce more cash flow. Get stuck on repeat.

*Choose a job you love, and you will never have to work a day in your life.*

*– Confucius*

Seventeen

# Power Up Your Purpose

***Challenge:*** *Go out of your way to do something during your day that exercises your true ambition. Walk in that purpose, and encourage coworkers to do the same.*

---

WHEN WE ARE AT WORK, we are often most concerned with making sure we perform our jobs to the best of our ability. These days, if you want to stay employed, you have to not only produce quality work, but exceed goals as well. We are operating for the benefit of keeping our jobs so that the bills get paid and we can continue to live the lifestyle to which we've become accustomed. As we go through our day to day, we must understand that there is more to our jobs than just doing good work. Using our purpose while at work gives us an opportunity for greater personal development and fulfillment.

Before we get deep into utilizing your purpose in the workplace, let's first identify what purpose is. Merriam-Webster defines purpose as "the reason why something is done or used; the aim or intention of something. The aim or goal of a person; what they are trying to do, become, etc." When you are truly operating in your purpose, you are intentionally using your gifts to become something greater.

Some people are well into their adulthood and have yet to discover what their purpose is. If you haven't been able to tap into your core to

*Personal, Professional, and Positive*

expose what powers you possess, then it is quite difficult to understand how you can make a difference. Many of us find our purpose through trial and error. Over time, you may experience a shift in your gifts. Because of experiences and deeper understanding, you may trade one purpose for another.

Make no mistake—we all have a purpose. It is our desire for determination that can create major momentum in our lives. When you are able to tap into the power within and understand why you are here and for what purpose, you can go into the world and shine your light on others. When we are acting in our purpose, it can be like being a flashlight for people, lighting up the darkness. You are able to lead with brightness and expose pathways that enlighten minds.

I believe the Dalai Lama said it best: "Our prime purpose in life is to help others. And if you can't help them, at least don't hurt them." Being purposeful is a self-given assignment—it is a choice. You can also elect to not use that powerful energy source and let it lie dormant, but successful people almost always utilize their passions and their purpose, because they understand that their success can have a positive affect on others.

So how can you use your purpose while at work? Living your purpose means that you don't shut it off just because you are working for someone else. If anything, it should put you in the prime position to help others and change lives. The workplace is just one place where we need more synergy and deeper thinking. If more employees are being purposeful, it can give the entire company the edge.

Here are three ways you can use your purpose while at work:

## Power Up Your Purpose

### 1. Make your actions your calling card.

When you lead by example and are a person of your word, then your actions speak powerfully. You become the person in the office to go to. When it comes to navigating through sticky situations or being the voice of reason, because you are a formidable employee, you are much respected and sought after, even if you aren't in a management position. This can help you move up the corporate ladder, which can bode well for your purpose. The higher your role, the more you can make your purpose a part of your role.

### 2. Assume a leadership role.

Even if you aren't in a management position, you can still lead. We all have different leadership styles, but leading in an authentic fashion without being bullish and heavy-handed usually gets the best results. You can lead quietly by offering suggestions without asking, helping others without expecting something in return, and being the voice of reason during conflicts or debates. With this leadership role, you can begin to exercise your purpose. For example, my purpose is to help others in need. By sharing my story and getting to know people on my team, I would be able to know who needed help and how I could assist them. You can easily work your purpose into the workplace by showcasing it while leading others. This is also a good way to get noticed for other roles of authority within the office.

### 3. Reach out and pull others up.

Whatever your purpose is, you aren't an island. When you reach out and pull others up with you, you are looked upon as someone people can trust and you are then considered a person worth knowing. One of the greatest assets you can be is someone others want to get to know; this will give you the opportunity to share your purpose as well.

*Personal, Professional, and Positive*

> ☞ **Professional Hack**
> Not sure where to start? You can begin with committees or service organizations within your employment to help you serve in a purposeful way. Talk to your HR department to get a list of events or volunteer opportunities that are available.

Being truly purposeful isn't about having a personal agenda. Motivational speaker Wayne Dyer said this about purposeful living: "When you dance, your purpose is not to get people on the dance floor. It's to enjoy each step along the way." Enjoy your career and profession. Be likeable, and work well with your colleagues and coworkers. Act in a manner that only allows people to treat you with the utmost respect. Be a game-changer who is highly motivated and only specializes in results. Your purpose distinguishes you from those who aren't living up to their full potential.

Don't shy away from your calling just because you are at work. If anything, use it to excel. Use it boldly to grow professionally and personally. Your mission, if you choose to accept it, is to live life by your design through your purpose. Powering up your passions begets purposeful living on the clock and off.

*Efforts and courage are not enough without purpose and direction.*

– *John F. Kennedy*

Eighteen

# A Wake-up Call to Excellence

***Challenge:*** *Look for examples of successful people who all have the same career to identify various attributes that help you raise the bar against your most nagging temptation to take shortcuts.*

---

THERE ARE PARTS OF YOU that just want to have fun, be entertained, and relax in coziness. One of man's greatest temptations is comfort. There is nothing wrong with that, except that it breeds a "middle of the road" mentality. You can be comfortable or courageous, but you cannot be both. If you desire to be a person of excellence you must confront mediocrity face to face.

One of the easiest things to do at work is get complacent. Mediocrity marches up and down the rows between cubicles, and many fall into its trap. We can subscribe to mindsets like these without knowing. There is a distant danger in doing an average job at work—it's called demotion. This is preventable if we start to look at mediocrity like a thief stealing away opportunities. Always beware of a "good-enough" attitude on the job. None of us can afford to stop challenging ourselves.

Tap into the boldness inside you to ask for greater responsibility and smarter assignments in the office. But be careful of what you ask for. Don't ask for anything you can't handle. If you can handle the task, step up to the plate and knock it out of the park!

*Personal, Professional, and Positive*

Here are the 10 Complacency Commandments:

1. Thou shalt not conform to office mediocrity.
2. Thou shalt not speak negatively of thyself.
3. Thou shalt commit to deadlines.
4. Thou shalt not feed into water-cooler gossip (sometimes you have to unfollow people in real life).
5. Thou shalt not lower thy standards.
6. Thou shall adhere to values, principles, and morals.
7. Thou shalt not let others (including your smartphone) break thy focus.
8. Thou shalt surround thyself with people smarter than thou.
9. Thou shalt refuse the temptation of shortcuts.
10. Thou shalt read the autobiographies of successful people.

> ☞ **Professional Hack**
> Mentor someone. There's no better way to learn and practice excellence than to teach others. Is there someone who can benefit from your help? Watch mediocrity disappear in both of your lives.

Mediocrity is a relentless monster that preys on the immature. At times our outer lives may be flourishing but inside some of us are in a state of infancy. If you don't put away mediocrity, it will put you away. It will put away promotion, progress, and prosperity. We must get back to principles that continue to foster growth. We should desire to be people that exude manners, morality, respect, trust, character, love, class, and integrity on the job. Your professional life today is the sum total of the decisions you've made yesterday.

## A Wake-up Call to Excellence

So what's it going to be? Mastery or mediocrity? Even if you achieve excellence today it inevitably becomes tomorrow's mediocrity. This is why you must pursue it on a daily basis. Seven days a week, twelve months per year. In a 'do whatever you will' type of world, self-discipline has become a taboo topic. Yet it is the chief practice and main ingredient to excellence. What habits do you need to develop to gain the life you want? Scan the mind and body to expose healthy habits from toxic ones. Some habits may not be exactly toxic; however, if it isn't producing fruit, it must go as well.

You will never achieve what you are capable of if you are too attached to the things you're supposed to let go of. It's all about creating good habits; afterward you no longer need discipline in that area. You move on to the next jacked-up part of your life. Let's view excellence as a journey, not a destination. While traveling this journey you may stray off the path, but don't get discouraged. Bounce back! Far too long you have settled for far too long. It's time to turn up.

*We should all be unsatisfied with mimicking the popular rather than mining the fertile veins of creativity that God placed deep with each of us.*

– Stewart Scott

Nineteen

# The Incredible Power of Concentration

***Challenge:*** *Create a private workspace with a quiet atmosphere conducive to clarity. This will assist in spotlighting the focal point of your work.*

WE CURRENTLY LIVE AN INFORMATION age with access to intelligence at our fingertips. Our world is also filled with enormous amounts of advertisements. Companies are lobbying for your undivided attention regardless of what your personal or professional pursuit is. However, your success is determined by what you are willing to ignore. What breaks your focus the easiest?

The #1 enemy to your goals is distraction. The more focused you are, the more intense the clarity of your goals. We like to be constantly entertained. We are fanatics about sporting events, concerts, surfing the web, eating, etc. There is nothing wrong with these things in moderation, but are we obsessing over the wrong things? I don't know about you, but I bore fairly easy, and had to learn to regulate myself when my attention was snagged away from priorities. I embraced the principle that you either suffer the pain of discipline, or the pain of regret. This life is much too short for regrets.

You produce what you focus on, good or bad. So make sure you are tuned in to the appropriate channels of life. Don't be afraid to switch paths or pave a new one when it makes sense. If you've been guaranteed to be on the right path, get as aggressive as a bulldog on your task. I need you to understand that you cannot be passive when combating distraction. The thing trying to knock you off your path is absolutely relentless and incredibly consistent. You literally have to wage war on seeds of procrastination. If they aren't destroyed, those seeds will grow roots, and with time produce fruits of failure. Good things don't come to those who wait: they come to those who work on meaningful goals. This requires a tremendous amount of self-denial.

Some things must be shifted and become nonnegotiable. The word "no" is a very liberating one, and can be your best asset while in pursuit of a goal. For a limited amount of time, it will be imperative that you turn your back on anything attempting to derail you. That phone call can wait. Your friends can wait. Food can wait, and believe it or not, Facebook and Twitter will be there when you return. You have to prepare yourself and your environment to create an atmosphere of focus. An atmosphere of peace. Surround yourself with all the tools you'll need to get the job done. Preparation will ultimately determine destination.

Out of all the voices calling out to you, which will you listen to? Your vision can keep you motivated and can keep you from breaking focus. Are your goals before your eyes? If you don't know where you are headed, any road you choose will take you there! Develop your focus as direct as a laser beam, and always remember how these three factors affect us:

**People:** anyone not leading you toward greater commitment is leading you from it.

**Direction:** always keep pictures of where you are going in front of and around you. There is a reason they put blinders on horses.

*Personal, Professional, and Positive*

**Time:** you don't have a lot of it, so spend its wealth wisely. Greater focus will open up more time; distractions will steal time away.

> ☞ **Professional Hack**
> Visit your local health-food store and purchase supplements for added brain power. Ginkgo biloba, Lecithin, and Omega 3 fish oils all are proven to boost your mental concentration.

I often hear professionals brag on their multitasking skills. Multitasking has its place, but you cannot rely on it. It's like putting $1 in a vending machine still expecting your $2 drink to be dispensed. Sure, you can juggle three things at once and get all three done, but how precise will you be? Are you willing to sacrifice quality? We must certainly be a more detailed people. Paying attention to the little things can yield many benefits in various parts of our lives, not just on the job. People begin to notice when an individual is meticulous about a subject. Don't you? Friends, life is won or lost in the details.

Put your assignment under the microscope. Study it. Ask yourself, what are the consequences of not completing the task you're working on? If you've wavered, it's okay. You can get back on track! Take control of your attention span. It's no walk in the park, but the fact remains that building and maintaining consistency is the key. Regaining your focus is much harder than maintaining your focus. The difference between your dreams and reality is action. When you begin to focus and attack tasks, the pressure of mediocrity will cease.

*The successful warrior is the average man, with laser-like focus.*

*– Bruce Lee*

Twenty

# Iron Sharpens Iron (Masterminds)

**Challenge:** *Identify, research, and join a mutually beneficial mastermind group, or start one yourself.*

---

NO MAN IS AN ISLAND. As the saying goes, two heads are better than one. We may have ideas that can help us get to the next level but it may take more than your ideas to make a difference professionally. Getting tips from others while receiving feedback on your ideas outfits you better for positive forward progression. Being a member of a professional mastermind group (MMG) can take you from zero to one hundred, while giving you the "thought capital" it takes to make super-smart decisions. Author and Personal Development Hero Napoleon Hill is attributed to coining the phrase Mastermind Group and cultivating it as an enrichment tool for professional growth.

Think of a mastermind group as a knife sharpener. Naturally, you have the ability to cut through the competition. However, there is a mutual benefit in the rubbing of two blades together. The edges become sharper and more efficient in their efforts. It is the support, networking, and accountability of a MMG that can help sharpen your skills making you a more consistent bladesmith in the boardroom. These are the kind of effects accountability groups can have.

The Success Alliance defines a mastermind group as "a combination of brainstorming, education, peer accountability, and support in a group setting." The group works together to help one another achieve ultimate success. These organizations have been around for over seventy-five years, but recently have gotten a lot of buzz due to online marketing and personal branding gaining a heavy market share. Masterminds are currently the soup de jour, and there are millions of people participating in them. They are consistently garnering positive results.

Participating in a peer-brainstorming group is like having your own personal board of directors, but without the pomp and circumstance or shares of stock. You have a group of individuals, usually entrepreneurs or professionals, whom you can consult on a consistent basis. They can act as a sounding board and play devil's advocate when needed. It is an asset that can help to raise your bar to heights you may have found difficult before.

> **Professional Hack**
> Use Meetup.com to meet like-minded people in your career field or genre. From those connections, establish your very own mastermind group.

In order to get an ultimate benefit out of your Round Table, you need to be active and consistent. If you aren't fully tapping into the potential of the team, then you won't be able to reap the rewards and the positive results. Make it a point to commit to the group wholeheartedly and participate in its goings-on.

Most mastermind groups are virtual and are accessed online. You can search the web for accountability groups that are a good fit, or you can ask your friends and colleagues for recommendations. Facebook is also a great place to search for a group, since there are millions of group pages available and open to the public. There are mastermind groups that are free of charge, as well as ones that cost money to be a part of. These groups are usually those run by a professional with excellent credentials and a list

## Iron Sharpens Iron (Masterminds)

of satisfied clients.

You can also create your own brain trust if you are unable to find one to be a part of. Simply create a group page, invite people whoms you'd like to join, set up guidelines for it, and voila! You now have your very own faction.

In a true mastermind group, there is no one leader. If you are the founder, you are ultimately there to make sure that everyone follows the guidelines. The association is about the group, not the founder of the group, so keep that in mind.

It is also a good idea to have an association full of different levels of expertise. For instance, you may have an accountant in the group. When questions or issues arise about accounting and money, they are the go-to person. You may also have a social media expert who can help answer questions and give advice about social networking for your business. The best groups are those that are well rounded and diverse in skills and execution.

There is power in singularity, and there is nothing wrong with depending on your own efforts for success. However, most people didn't do it alone. Consider the legacies of Kobe Bryant without a Shaquille O'Neal, or Michael Jordan without a Scottie Pippen. When you align yourselves with other successful people who have a hunger for greatness, you are destined to do well. By extending your network and collaborating with others, the sky's the limit.

*Alone, we can do so little; together, we can do so much.*

*– Helen Keller*

# III. Positive

Twenty-One

# Random Acts of Kindness

**Challenge:** *The next time you are passing through a toll booth, pay for the car behind you.*

---

THERE IS NO BETTER FEELING in the world than to be a blessing to someone else. The old adage It is better to give than to receive isn't limited to holidays and birthdays. When acts of kindness toward others become a lifestyle our own lives seem to get set on autopilot. It's really important to be a good person. Period. When love becomes the answer to all issues, the power locked in our relationships will manifest much more often. Let's consider people more. Let's think the best about people. Start people out at 100%, no judgments.

Many years ago, I sat in an audience and listened a speaker talk about how she loves to pay for the person behind her after stopping at a toll both. She began to do the same at grocery stores and restaurants. I was blown away, and couldn't believe people like this existed. I began to experiment with random acts of kindness with astonishing results. The super cool part is oftentimes there is a domino effect. When a person is on the receiving end of a kind act, they tend to show it to the next person and so on. You can almost see each person jolted with shock and excitement. They were surprised that anyone would be so kind, and were excited to do the same. I love to take a $100 bill, change it into five $20 dollar bills, and randomly distribute them to the homeless I pass on my way to work.

*Personal, Professional, and Positive*

It isn't about making you feel great about yourself; it's a simple understanding that people need people. Without you, there is no me. I don't need to know who you are or what your story is to put a smile on your face. Happiness is not found—it's created. Acts of kindness can have a lifelong effect on people.

I will probably never forget when I was eight years old. My birthday came, and no one seemed to know or care. In the late afternoon, my cousin came home from school with a small toy for me, and I was the happiest kid in the world. It's in these moments when you feel like no one else cares when kindness will shine through. I'm now in my thirties, but that moment will live in my heart forever.

> **☞ Positive Hack**
> Write an online review of a positive experience you've had with a worker who helped you greatly while you shopped or ate.

Celebrate others. Even the humblest of people like to be recognized. The feeling we get knowing someone went out of their way to acknowledge a milestone or an achievement often cannot be described. It shows that what is important to them is also important to you. When my grandmother turned ninety years old, I began to realize that I didn't have much more time left with her. The family decided to have a celebration for her, and to present a beautiful crystal award as a symbol of gratitude for raising generations of children. I can only image how this made her feel. Now that she is no longer with us, I'm glad we showed such appreciation.

Congratulate others—even when you don't want to. Let's be honest: there are days when we don't feel our best. Days when you want to be left alone. Since living a selfless life isn't about us, it takes an extra portion of will and grace to push through how we feel, and to bless others. Solving someone else's problem in the midst of your own struggles requires a significant amount of humility. It's the same humility you show when you give up your lifestyle after having your first child.

Even when you don't feel like being nice, the beautiful part is that it comes back to you. Sometimes we want to help others but just can't. In those situations, you can pray for your loved one. It doesn't cost a dime; just a moment of quiet time. When your friend pops up in your head, that's God trying to get you to pray for your friend. You may think this person is on your mind randomly, but this is no coincidence. You begin to notice that people come to your rescue when you, in turn, need a helping hand. When you need a listening ear or a shoulder to cry on, you won't be forsaken.

Life is a series of stories, and the way our stories intersect is remarkable! Small acts performed by millions of people can transform the world. Here are some ideas to get you started:

- Buy a coworker a coffee.
- Help a neighbor with yard work.
- Encourage your child to set up a free lemonade stand.
- Have a free garage sale.
- Visit a nursing home.
- Pray with someone.
- Wash your mom's car.

If you are asked for aid, don't lend; give. If it won't hurt, give the help they are looking for without expecting repayment. Look at it as a

## Personal, Professional, and Positive

gift instead of a loan. That way you aren't expecting payback, excluding possible drama. When it's in your power to help someone, do it with urgency. Be quick to help. Be quick to be kind. Be quick to resist any "what's is in it for me" attitudes.

Always remember, we must serve people with our gifts. Those who refresh others will be refreshed themselves. If you are not fulfilled, you are possibly doing more taking in than giving away. That's like inhaling without exhaling, and you know what happens then—you stop breathing. You shouldn't need a reason to help someone. Each of us has a specific purpose and a job to do but we rise by lifting each other up. No act of kindness, no matter how small, is ever wasted. No beauty shines brighter than that of a good heart.

*Generosity is the most natural outward expression of an inner attitude of*

*compassion and loving- kindness.*

*–Dalai Lama*

Twenty-Two

# Lend a Listening Ear

***Challenge:*** *Pay attention to your body language when you listen. Lean in, give eye contact, and nod. Train yourself to listen with your whole body, not just your ears.*

---

THE PREVIOUS CHAPTER ENCOURAGES US to lend a helping hand, but it is also important to lend a listening ear. We all think we do a good job of hearing people out, when in reality most of us are failures at being attentive. There is a big difference between hearing and listening. Hearing without listening is like conversing in a foreign language. If you don't speak the language, then you are hearing the conversation with zero comprehension. Our ears are open twenty-four hours a day—we can't physically turn them off and on. However, you can activate our minds to convert what you've heard into what you know.

When we first hear sound, it has entered our eardrums on its way to our brain. Once our minds receive sound, we decide if we are going to pay active attention to it. Eventually our attention is captured. We then begin to understand, take what's meaningful, and apply it in the situation's context. Lastly, we store the information in our memory files. This is the technical cerebral process of listening. But unfortunately, many of us never move from that initial hearing stage.

## *Personal, Professional, and Positive*

Think about the last time you had a problem that you needed to discuss. As you were talking to this person, did you feel like they were listening? Did they give you verbal clues that they were tuned in totally? If you were speaking in person, did they give you eye contact? Did you feel like you were being ignored? In some of our two-way conversations, pride often wants to rear its evil head. When wanting to get a point across, we don't actively hear what the other person is saying—we are just waiting for our turn.

Many of the situations we find ourselves in would be eliminated, or at least reduced if we listened more. I find this especially true when it comes to relationships. We often "hear" things that weren't said through misinterpretation or misunderstanding, which can breed other issues. These sorts of problems tend to pile on top of one another. If we listened more actively, perhaps some of these situations could be avoided.

Listening is also a form of respect and a can be an act of love. It can be difficult to respond to a friend who is struggling emotionally. It takes practice to become a skilled listener. However, staying locked into the cares of others requires a compassionate heart. Being an active listener means being fully engaged, tuned in to what's at hand, and tuned out of interferences. We aren't looking at our phones, or playing on the Internet. When you are an active listener, you not only make the person you are speaking with comfortable, but you give attention to their words with your replies and non-verbal actions. You acknowledge their pauses, make eye contact, and respond to their cadence.

Here are some keys to being a better listener and effective communicator:

## Lend a Listening Ear

1. Repeat the person for clarification. One of the most powerful ways to express that you are paying attention is to summarize what you've heard. When we are gaining an understanding of the speaker, we will memorize important points to discuss later. It acknowledges feelings, expresses sympathy, and confirms understanding. A prompt like "Let me see if I understand this correctly" can really help foster the conversation, and helps you really home in on what the person is saying. It's a good exercise to use during conversations to make sure if you are on the same page.
2. Don't be defensive. We often get defensive, which doesn't allow us to concentrate. We begin to get wrapped up in what we feel. There is no need for defense if others aren't truly being offensive. Even if they are, be the bigger person and inject love into the conversation.
3. Keep positive body language. Good listeners also focus on the person they are speaking to. Eye contact is extremely important.
4. Don't be so quick to respond. After the person is done speaking, you don't have to say something right away. Process what they've said to you, restate it if necessary, then reply with your carefully considered thoughts. Good listeners think before they speak.

> **☞ Positive Hack**
> Follow up with those you've had meaningful conversations with. Getting an update shows you care. A good listener will follow up later with ideas, questions, or facts to add value.

*Personal, Professional, and Positive*

Being a good and active listener is a trait research has found amongst true leaders and visionaries. They tend to actively engage others and listen more than they speak. According to Virgin Group CEO Sir Richard Branson, if you want to be a good leader, you have to be a good listener: "Brilliant ideas can spring from the most unlikely places, so you should always keep your ears open for some shrewd advice. Get out there, listen to people, draw people out, and learn from them."

In our over-scheduled society, we've lost the art of listening. Being a good and active listener makes you an asset. It's a powerful habit that will separate you from the pack. With this quality, you can help others sidestep pitfalls and arrive at solutions unscathed. This a very positive habit to form, one that generally doesn't go unnoticed. So many of us are too distracted to focus on others. When we lock in, we show the respect we'd also like to see when communicating our own cares.

*Speak in such a way people love to listen to you.*

*Listen in such a way people want to speak to you.*

*– Anonymous*

Twenty-Three

# The Power of Words

***Challenge:*** *Whenever someone greets you and asks how you're doing, answer with "grand," "splendid," or "marvelous." This will remind you that life really is great as well as uplift the state of the person asking.*

---

IF YOU HAD TO BE held accountable for every single word you've ever spoken, would you think before you speak? Many of us grew up believing the old phrase Sticks and stones may break bones, but words can't ever hurt me. I can assure you this cute phrase is a lie. In fact, the words we choose to speak are packed with creative power. Power to construct, design, and organize the world around you. They have to potential to crush hearts, as well as mend them. The capability to shatter dreams or stimulate them. They can create resistance or melt it.

Use your words to release your faith. Literally opening your mouth and confessing what you are hoping for helps to establish it. Situations have to respect the authority you possess over it. Speaking good tidings into our surroundings pumps them full of positivity. The walls of uncertainty begin to crumble, leaving only the foundation of faith you've created. You can now begin to build the world you always wanted.

The articulation of your faith is vital. Your words will act as a waiter, bringing the fruit of what your lips have ordered. If you sow words of love, peace, and kindness, then you will reap these qualities. If you sow words of sickness, fear, doubt, and worry, then you will reap those things.

*Personal, Professional, and Positive*

We must control any temptation to tear others down with our words. Soft words create friends; harsh words create enemies. Don't use your words to claim things you actually don't want in your life. I'm going to use the classic phrase "I'm sick," for example. This two-word phrase is laying claim to an undesirable condition. Never say anything about yourself that you don't want to come true.

To correct this behavior, you first have to notice and identify when you are using your words negatively. Once you are in the habit of spotting it, you will be able to consistently combat them with uplifting words of encouragement and faith.

Here are some quick dos and a couple of don'ts when using our words:

- **Do:** Use your words for accountability. Help people stand for what they believe in.
- **Don't:** Use your words to doubt yourself. Use words to create positive thoughts about yourself.
- **Do:** Use your words for truth. Lies aren't worth the trouble. More clarity=less confusion.
- **Don't:** Use your words to complain. Even if you have a right to complain, it won't help at all.
- **Do:** Think before you speak. Spoken thoughts reveal who you really are.
- **Don't:** Be a hater. Blowing out someone else's candle doesn't make yours shine any brighter.
- **Do:** Be cool. A gentle answer turns away wrath, but harsh words continue to stir up anger.
- **Don't:** Lie to people that trust you, and don't trust people that lie to you.

## The Power of Words

> ☞ **Positive Hack**
> Develop a list of alternatives to any negative words you may use. Rely on your own intelligence and select a few faithful or even funny words, and get in the habit of substituting them.

We've replaced the proper terms for things with vulgar, ugly, and disrespectful words. Many of us were taught or heard bad words growing up, and naturally adopted them as the norm. This habit could have been passed down for generations, but it can stop with you. Don't ever be loyal to dysfunction. I use to curse like a sailor, but I learned that a person is known by their words just as much as the company they keep. Now I cringe when I hear certain words. Obscenities, swearing, cursing, blasphemy, and profanity are all marks of lower social stratification. It is discourteous to haphazardly spew foul language without a filter. These words don't elevate; they pull down. I know this may offend some, but if you can look past emotion I believe you'll agree that replacing rude words with positive ones adds value to everyone.

After discovering my words were powerful enough to create as well as destroy, I made a choice to speak life into dead situations. My circumstances now obey my words and faith about an issue. You can begin to detoxify yourself of cursing and words of doubt today.

Expand your vocabulary. You should never be satisfied with what you currently know. A lack of vocabulary can hinder you greatly. Improving the quality of our words can increase the quality of our lives. Do you own a prescriptive paperback dictionary or thesaurus? If so, dust it off and revisit its knowledge. Find better, more intellectual words to mediate on.

*Personal, Professional, and Positive*

Your mind will eventually begin to select the correct words for you. As an educated adult, you know bigger words; use them. Read as much as you can. Get into the good habit of purchasing hard-copy books, listening to lectures, and sitting in on speeches. Choose a word of the day, explore its history, and use it correctly throughout the week.

*Watch your thoughts, they become words; watch your words, they become actions; watch your actions, they become habits; watch your habits, they become character; watch your character, for it becomes your destiny.*

*— Frank Outlaw*

Twenty-Four

# Living the Positive Thought Life

**Challenge:** *Overload your brain with positivity through one book, one podcast, and one video all in one day. This will flush negativity you weren't even aware of out.*

CLOSE TO FIFTY THOUSAND THOUGHTS pass through our minds on a daily bases. Our current lives equal the total sum of our thoughts. We are delighted with warm thoughts of love and laughter. In the same breath, we are troubled by thoughts of worry and fear. Good or bad, each thought must pass through a checkpoint to filter those that have the ability to negatively affect our lives. Allowing bogus thoughts to go unchecked can cause you to mildly obsess about them, which often leads to stress, anxiety, and, ultimately, bad decisions.

This is a rarely practiced, under-discussed, yet necessary topic to tackle. It's not your circumstances that determine your thoughts, it's your thoughts that determine your circumstances. Once you have an experience, your brain will file it in the back of your mind. If a similar situation arises, your brain automatically pulls those past thoughts back to the forefront. Mentally, we should desire a state where our first reaction is a thought of faith. Thoughtfully prepare to face situations head on with a positive attitude. You have the ability to choose what you are going to contemplate, and what you are inundated with. This is how you begin to

*Personal, Professional, and Positive*

creatively force your brain to a different, more positive alternative. You have to fight for your right to a positive life!

Misfortunes can consume our thought life, producing negative, reoccurring thoughts. We should never naively underestimate how powerful negativity is. Taking a stand against negativity takes bravery. We would be remiss if we allowed our thoughts to run wild. The mature in spirit will condition themselves to arrest renegade thoughts. If I continuously contemplate the last hurdle I was unable to clear, it can hinder the success of jumping over the next one.

How can you tell if you need to exchange bad thoughts for positive ones? How does one wrangle up all of the negative ones? Just pay attention to the things you say. Listen to yourself. Are you using words of faith or words of worry? Through what kind of lens are we looking at our lives? Do you look at the light at the end of the tunnel, or focus on the crack in the Mona Lisa? Start documenting your thoughts. Jot down thoughts as they come. This will show a string of positive or negative thoughts. At the end of your day, take twenty minutes to take a look at the list and see if there is an unfavorable pattern of thinking.

Begin to take notice of the thoughts that pass through your mind. Ask yourself if this is a thought that will help or hinder? Where did you come from? A person, TV advertising? Yourself? If it is negative, you must redirect it. You'll get to a place where you can quickly pinpoint the thought. Once you've identified it, your best line of defense is your mouth. Use your mouth to conquer your mind. If you don't literally open your mouth and speak directly to the thought, then you reestablish it. By recognizing your triggers, you'll have something concrete to work with. Think about how many times you've worried about the possibility of an outcome, only to realize it never happened. There is absolutely no future in worry. It is a huge waste of time.

Recently a friend needed to meet up for a drink and vent about a bad day. Right before an important job interview, he locked himself out of his car and home. He called Uber for a ride, only to arrive forty-five minutes late. He was borderline depressed and convinced himself he wouldn't get a return call. Yet, he got the job! I believe he also had the revelation that no matter how dire the situation, we don't know the outcome, so why worry? The best thing to do is activate faith, speak positive words over the situation, and resist thoughts of worry.

> **☞ Positive Hack**
> Wear a rubber band on your wrist. Each time you catch yourself thinking negatively, pull the band back, and snap it. A little pain reconditions the brain to avoid these thoughts.

They say the eyes are the window to the soul. Our bodies are equipped with a various gates of entry. Not only our eyes, but our mouths and ears are receptors as well. Are you mindful of what you listen to? Faith begins to develop by listening to something over and over again. Are you indulging in an abundance of reality television programs? I hope not, because it's just that—programming. What types of content fills your YouTube and Instagram accounts? Protecting your spirit from contamination is not to be taken lightly. If what you are allowing in these gates are tipping the scales of negativity, do not expect to see positivity show up at your door.

Plenty of people think this isn't an issue. I agree to a certain extent that these things are entertainment, but you have to understand that it

## Personal, Professional, and Positive

will be some kind of impact. I know adults that have walked into a horror movie and couldn't go to sleep that night. Some things are beyond your conscious. The images and sounds we let inside of us can certainly cause involuntary responses and urges. Beware of overthinking; you don't want to think your way out of opportunities and into worry.

Positivity isn't popular, but it is important. There are many benefits of positive thinking. Some include reduced levels of anxiety and depression, increased physical well-being, and enlightenment. The manifestation of these types of things in our lives are what we need. You can also become a bolder individual after knocking down the walls of woe. Changing your mindset can get you in a mood where you are feeling like there isn't anything you can't overpower. The key to real happiness is a bit more complicated than just thinking positive. But that is where it starts! The mind is very similar to a parachute; it doesn't work very well unless it's open.

*Finally, brothers and sisters, whatever is true, whatever is noble, whatever is right, whatever is pure, whatever is lovely, whatever is admirable— if anything is excellent or praiseworthy—think about such things.*

*– Paul the Apostle*

Twenty-Five

# An Environment of Encouragement

***Challenge:*** *The very next time you see someone on your Facebook timeline express sorrow over bad news, send them a direct inbox message of encouragement. Keep it short, positive, and opinion free.*

---

ONE OF MY PERSONAL HEROES, the late author and speaker Stephen R. Covey, said it best: "Treat a man as he is and he will remain as he is. Treat a man as he can and should be and he will become as he can and should be." There is something wonderful and brilliant about giving someone a boost when misfortune abounds. Our cities are jam-packed with people, yet so many feel lost and alone. Giving someone the gentle nudge of positive words can make a world of difference. As mentioned in a previous chapter, the words we ingest and share are important. It can make a true difference and be a blessing to someone who may need a hearty pep talk to help them stay on track.

Have you ever been the person in need of a few words of consolation? When someone was right there to share a dose of inspiration, how important was that to you? It probably meant a lot to have someone in your corner, giving you supportive solace when you really needed it. Perhaps it wasn't words, but their presence that saw you through. We all need people in our lives to be a beacon of light.

*Personal, Professional, and Positive*

Lending your time or offering aid can be a shot in the arm to someone in distress. It's an act of the heart that someone will be hard-pressed to forget. Most of us can point to a time when someone swooped in like superman to save our day. Maybe we should be a constant source of encouragement for our fellow man. You know how your friend or family member can stay on your mind all week?

I've heard it be said that if someone pops into your mind repeatedly, you should immediately reach out to them. There is a reason these thoughts invade your mind. When this happens, be prepared to encourage, enlighten, and simply listen and be there. Even if they aren't going through a difficult or challenging time, your advocacy can bring comfort.

There are simple things that you can do to uplift others. Here are a few suggestions that will bring smiles of hope across the faces of fear and disappointment:

1. Notes aren't dead: Mail a card or note with a few words showing that they are on your heart and your mind. It is also a practice that we have fallen away from in this digital age, but always shows thoughtfulness and personalization.
2. Rewind and remind: When speaking to someone in need of loving words, make sure to remind them of all of the wonderful and great qualities they possess. Sometimes we can forget about the traits we have been blessed with, but a good friend is always there to remind us.
3. Find how to help: Oftentimes, asking someone how you can help him or her will go a long way. They may be feeling like no one cares. Being proactive in asking them how you can help may persuade them to open up to you.

## An Environment of Encouragement

4. Share your story: Strength can be contagious. You can help strengthen others by showing yours. When people get to hear that others have experienced something similar, they know they aren't alone and hope floods in.

> **☞ Positive Hack**
> Next time you are out for dinner and receive good service from an employee, make sure to let their boss know that they did a good job.

When you are helping from the heart, you can easily forget about all the good you've done for others. Then when we face an unfavorable situation, we often need to be advised of what's pleasant and positive instead of the bad and ugly. So while you are encouraging others, don't forget to encourage yourself as well. You may have to muster motivation from within, as we cannot always rely on others. Regularly write down your personal affirmations and read them on days you experience adversity. Keep your confirmations close so you can refer to them at a moment's notice.

Our aim is to encourage you to eagerly encourage others in obvious need. Encourage others to act when there is an injustice. Encourage others to conserve energy, limit waste, and recycle. Encourage others to reach deep within themselves to pull out the excellence that is lying dormant. Make this a new personal habit, if it isn't already.

Emphasize all the good and what they do correctly when they're zoned out about bad tidings. Be quick to point them to evidence of the seeds they've sown in the past, reminding them of a soon-to-come harvest.

*Personal, Professional, and Positive*

Express that you understand how they may feel. Your mere presence lets them know they aren't alone. People will ultimately respond to positivity. It may or may not seem like it at first, but they are receiving the message. Don't kill them with kindness—heal them with kindness. Love is always the answer.

*No one is useless in this world who lightens the burdens of another.*

*– Charles Dickens*

Twenty-Six

# Order is Everything

**Challenge:** *Establish and celebrate a monthly "De-clutter day" for yourself. Pick one day each month where you reestablish and organize everything. Keep only what you need.*

---

ARE THERE POCKETS OF DISORDER in your life? If so, it may be time to put things into the proper perspective and the right order. With order comes clarity. When things aren't in their proper place mentally, physically, financially, and emotionally, our lives can drift off course. If our worlds are off balance, negativity creeps in through the cracks. You begin to speak negatively over yourself, and even agree when others do the same. Talk to highly successful people, and many will say that being organized was key to their achievement. There is something that can be said about an individual who makes a habit of keeping things in order, avoiding a chaotic environment.

When you are organized, you understand the importance of efficiency and subsequently avoid the mental slavery of procrastination. Think of that one friend who is always misplacing things, runs late for most appointments, and lacks tidiness. Because of this, they may be stressed. That doesn't contribute to a well-run lifestyle.

Having systems in place that keep a neat working space, a tidy home, and a de-cluttered environment goes a long way to positive fulfillment. Being dedicated to living a life without the additional stress of living

*Personal, Professional, and Positive*

amongst clutter brings clarity. With that, confidence and other positives are sure to overflow.

So how can you move toward a plan of structure?

First things first: living with less is the mission. Begin to access items that you don't use in your living spaces. Find things that you want to keep but aren't in use at the present time—think seasonal items and clothing. Box these up and put them away in storage. Things that you no longer have need for, donate to local organizations in your area or your church. You can even make a little extra spending money by holding a garage sale.

> ☞ **Positive Hack**
> Give everything an assigned place in your life. When things (including people) are out of their assigned place, you will create a habit of noticing and fixing it right away.

Next is your work area. Thoroughly clear your workspace of old papers. Recycle or use the shredder if disposing of sensitive or classified information. Do the same thing to your car. Get rid of trash and items that are taking up space inside your car and trunk. Use travel pouches for items that you want to keep in your automobile and keep them in the glove compartment or other storage space.

Bringing order to your existence is completely necessary to your health. Your body is a machine that needs maintenance to stay out of a state of disorder or disease. Place people in their proper categories and resist the temptation to clutter. We often put people in positions they were never meant to play. Levels of anxiety sink when you begin catalog people and priorities. Rank tasks in order of importance and manage them daily.

## Order is Everything

Being organized is an uplifting characteristic that can affect your personal and professional life. It can help you in ways that move you toward the goals you have set forth. When putting your best foot forward in a positive manner, managing one's living and working spaces is critical.

Until this becomes a habit, you may begin to notice things are starting to back up again if constancy is low. I'd like to recommend a thorough organizational touchup at least once a month for a healthier and simplistic lifestyle. Keep life simple. Simple is easy. Simple is less stressful. Living clean while cutting out all of the filler will help you step up your game and move closer toward your purpose. When you keep things uncomplicated, it can contribute to you being a more organized and positive person. Be transparent with yourself and decide if you need more order to your life.

*A place for everything, and everything in its place.*

*– Ben Franklin*

Twenty-Seven
# Defeat Won't Define Your Destiny

*Challenge:* Set up safety nets (financial, emotional, etc.) specific to your calling that will help bring you into alignment, especially if you have ever drifted away from destiny's path before.

How do you view yourself when you fail? When you fall—and we all do—do you dust yourself off and get right back on the horse? If you don't, each moment you stay off is a moment away from destiny. It's funny how even our defeats prepare us for our destiny. There are messages of correction, confirmation, and information within life's daily challenges. Difficulties often drive ordinary people into extraordinary circumstances. Just like anything else, it's all about how we look at things.

We can sometimes make the mistake of devaluing our worth when life gives us lemons. I'm not going to tell you to make lemonade. However, make sure your worst enemy isn't living between your own ears. We must never get into a habit of underestimating ourselves. Any voice in your head that says, "You can't do it" is lying to you. This thought is an enemy to excellence and smothers promise. One of my favorite books is Rich Dad, Poor Dad by financial literacy activist Robert Kiyosaki. In the book, Kiyosaki talks about how once you tell your mind "NO," you've stopped it from looking for ways to create or find a "YES."

Self-confidence is one of the most attractive qualities a person can have. People will begin to view you the way you view you. Learn to love yourself first, instead of loving the idea of other people loving you. Some may consider your uniqueness strange. If this is the case, that's fine, but do not allow anyone to speak negatively over you. Cut them off mid-sentence if you have to.

There is greatness in every person on Earth, and it is our duty to tap into it. We were all created with potential, and sometimes you have to put a demand on that potential. This means taking your current limitation and putting it on your agenda as a job to do. For example, if you have a desire to be a web designer but don't know code, you immerse yourself in all things tech. You aggressively educate yourself. You find mentors in the field and completely live it until the limitation becomes a skill. Are you doing what you believe in, or are you settling for what you are doing? Whatever it is you desire to do, your potential is boundless.

> **Positive Hack**
> Be open. Your destiny may take you down a road you've never considered before. Be flexible to opportunities off the beaten path; detours can turn into gold.

Our greatness isn't equipped with the absence of flaws, but it is loaded with your ability to push past them. Once you've accepted your flaws, no one can use them against you. It can be difficult not to get overwhelmed by your inadequacies, which is why it's important to speak words of positivity over yourself. This will help you get over your past and embrace your future. You are an outstanding design created by a gifted designer. You are strong, but you're stronger than you think. Of course you're bright, but you're even more intelligent than you think. You are complex, beautiful, and breathtaking to behold. We are remarkable beings that have the tendency to amaze ourselves at things we never knew we could do. When

## Personal, Professional, and Positive

you realize who are, you'll be surprised at what you are capable of. Have a little faith in yourself. Faith is like Wi-Fi: it's invisible but has the power to connect you to what you need.

A healthy optimism is acting positively while at the same time being realistic. Sure, we should have good expectations that positive things happen, but realistically this isn't always the case. Early in life we've learned that we don't get to have everything we desire. Mentally being ready for what might not work out prevents you from spiraling into the depths of disappointment. It's natural to question ourselves after a dampening event. But the negativity should end there. Beware of meditating on our wrongs, because it has the ability to convince us that dreams are dead.

Some of us have the tendency to beat ourselves up when we miss the mark. Some meet targets, some fall short. That's life. You have a couple of options here: let it define you, destroy you, or strengthen you. Some may see your mistakes as defeat, or your success accidental. No matter how many mistakes you make, you are still ahead of everyone who isn't trying. You're going to lose some people on the way; just remember that not everyone is intended to go with you.

Even when you feel sidelined, always know the world needs you. You are the salt that adds flavor to a bland world. Light is needed most when it's the darkest, so be the light in a dim situation. Destiny can hide you with one hand and reveal who you are with the other. How hard you press determines how far you go. The truth is, you won't possess what you won't passionately pursue. Stay the fight. You are much more than a conqueror. To conquer means to gain control of or subdue by strong force. It is with this force that you must meet your fails, making your wins all the sweeter.

*A person often meets his destiny on the road he took to avoid it.*

– Jean de la Bruyere

Twenty-Eight

# Patience is Worth the Wait

***Challenge:*** *Make a list of triggers that ignite impatience. Each time you identify where you should've shown more restraint, keep a tally on your sheet. This will visually aid you in improving over time.*

PATIENCE IS A POSITIVE TRAIT often commended but rarely practiced. Patience will bring a sense of peace of mind, body, and soul. A settling of the spirit develops a more balanced you. It's a behavior that shows a high level of moral standards, one our parents tried to instill in us early on. We've embedded our mind with statements like Good things come to those who wait or In good time. If we've been taught these virtues at an early age, why are we still so impatient?

As children we were often rewarded when we exercised patience. Perhaps it was a lollipop from the bank teller who praised us for being so sweet while our parents conducted business. We raised our hand in class in order to be called on by our teachers. Think about how extremely patient someone had to be with you when you were learning how to read, ride a bike, or drive a car. These were cues that we were to adopt as our own to foster calmness and restraint.

Your ability to show restraint can impact your relationship with your own child. If you display a lack of self-control, your child may also grow to develop those habits, which will then begin to cause issues in their lives. It's our job as parents to identify and confront bad habits before they are learned by the little ones.

*Personal, Professional, and Positive*

Wanting isn't bad, but demanding what we want, when we want it is childish and a bit prideful. Having patience shows you are humble enough to know that things take time and hardly ever revolve around your personal schedule. Patience has everything to do with attitude. Do you maintain a positive attitude while you wait for a specific want or need? Do you quickly become frustrated with the process of waiting? You are a very strong person. You can certainly endure the waiting process. The longer you have to wait for something, the more you will appreciate it when it shows up. Anything worth having is worth waiting for—would you agree?

Lending leniency to others is imperative to a positive lifestyle. People get so bent out of shape over frivolous inessentials. We have to keep our composure with people in times of frustration. Don't be that guy that submits himself to the trap of road rage, or that girl who is rude to a slow waitress. If you sow patience, you will reap patience. The day will come when you will need someone to direct tolerance your way.

> ☞ **Positive Hack**
> Catch up with your thoughts when you're at a "standstill." Count to five and slowly allow this to calm you, pressing your mental reset button.

If you struggle with restlessness, there is good news. There are ways to set the stage for apathy. Create a mental environment of preparedness. Be ready to respond with reason when situations arise.

**Press Reset:** If you are tempted to act or speak impulsively, stop to take a deep breath to reset. Do this a couple of times before making your next move. If you want to interrupt someone mid-sentence, if someone eats your last piece of pie, or cuts you off in traffic, it's okay to let it go. No

## Patience is Worth the Wait

harm, no foul. This simple act can help you avoid acting irrationally.

**Take Time:** Just like anything else, we gradually come into knowledge. It took you a certain length of ramp time to learn your job, and now you rock at it. Good relationships take time to develop, but the joy lies in the journey. It took time to pack on those pounds, and it's going to take time to drop them. It even takes time to unlearn the programming of bad habits. Never despise the day of small beginnings. Let time run its course, no more jumping out of the oven before you're done baking.

**Think First:** It is extremely important to make well-informed decisions. It is when we act on partial wisdom that we regret it. Take a moment to gather information, contemplate, and respond with wisdom rather than emotion.

**Delay Indulgence:** I know that bonus check that you just received could come in handy right now, but before you spend it, hold on to it if you can. Deposit it in the bank and if all of your outstanding bills are paid, let it sit there for a month or two. Resist urges to spend extra money. Making better choices of how and when to spend will eventually suppress impulsive thoughts and purchases.

**Have Faith:** It is necessary to let faith flourish and know that everything is going to work out, even if it doesn't work the way, or when you want it. Patience is a reaction to information we've processed concerning the precious currency of time. Exercising hope helps you know things will happen at their appointed time.

There are no real shortcuts in life. Sometimes we are too quick to sacrifice quality for convenience. In this instant age of overnight success, we want our meals in minutes and our movies on demand. We've come to

*Personal, Professional, and Positive*

tell you that there is a blessing in the waiting portion of a procedure. As we anticipate the arrival of a circumstance, certain characteristics begin to sprout inside you. Your endurance begins to expand, maturity multiplies, and strength seems to spread.

Practicing patience will prevent later regrets. Never allow the influences of a microwave society to sway self-control or compromise poise. There is no prosperity without patience. There are no awards without waiting. Being a person of patience will bear the fruit of good decision-making. Don't rush anything. When the time is right, it will happen!

*Patience is bitter, but its fruit is sweet.*

*– Aristotle*

Twenty-Nine

# Standing Strong in Storms

***Challenge:*** *Take a moment to reflect on the mentality you had in the middle of your last storm. Ask if your attitude at the time helped or hindered you.*

---

RAIN AND SUNSHINE BOTH HAVE a place in our lives, literally and figuratively. They each have seasons, as well as purposes. Are you currently facing an unexpected challenge in life? Webster's Dictionary defines storms as "a violent disturbance of the atmosphere." The reality is, you are not what you have done—you are what you have overcome. Overcomers operate in the realm of the uncommon. It is uncommon to stay the fight after unbelievable adversity. It is uncommon to seek wisdom, and then actually apply it. You beat some incredible odds just to be born, so your current struggle is the evidence of progress.

When it comes to the storms, sometimes the only way out is through. Think about it: If you were walking down the street and it began to downpour, you wouldn't just pause. You'd continue on to your destination faster, and endure the soaking of the raindrops. Sure, it would be great to run for cover, but sometimes the shelter isn't in reach. Some storms cannot be avoided, and some can. The good thing is that they are temporary. Remember, joy rides alongside each bright new day, waiting for you to tap in.

*Personal, Professional, and Positive*

It is super important to have a positive attitude, simply because someone is always watching us and gaining strength from what we go through. Life is a bowl of grapes. Some are good while others are rotten. It's your job to throw out the rotten ones and forget about them while you enjoy eating the ones that are good! This is something you must consider. Believe it or not, there is a blessing in the storm. This is why you shouldn't let a hard lesson harden your heart. Finding good cheer in the midst of chaos isn't easy, but complaining is counterproductive.

Mother Nature can present a plethora of storms, from tornadoes to floods to hurricanes. Natural disasters knock on our personal doors as well. Sometimes we aren't sure if we invited difficulties or if they've come on their own. It's important to take a humble step back and look in the mirror for a self-scan. Too often we are tempted to point the finger at external factors, when many times these challenges are self-imposed. Setbacks can arrive for a variety of reasons. Usually it's either to correct you or to perfect you.

*Corrective storms* come when you have drifted off track with a purpose of putting you back into the lane you may have wavered from. Years ago, I was horrible at managing my finances, launching me into a financial whirlwind. Although I'd brought this on myself, I stayed in this period for quite some time because I didn't diagnose the problem. Unfortunately, it took me hitting rock bottom before I began to educate myself on money management.

*Perfecting storms* come to make you stronger and bring the best out of you. There are levels to life and our paths have a way of catching us off guard, especially when things are well. Sometimes to go to that next level takes pain. When you are in the gym pumping iron, your strength can plateau if you don't regularly add more weight. The weights of life foster growth.

Growth in the things you love require testing. This is something we must not fear but embrace. If you are afraid of fear, it has the ability to paralyze and stop forward progress. What if everything you've ever dreamed of was on the other side of this test?

> **Positive Hack**
> Allow positive people, pictures, and words of inspiration to push you through rough times. Create a plan of escape and adjust your sails accordingly.

I remember injuring my leg to the point where I lost the ability to earn. This came directly after losing a parent, an uncle, an aunt, and a friend within a six-month span. I remember thinking, "How much can a person take in such a short amount of time?" and "God must really think I'm strong." As you can imagine, I was at an all-time low. I felt like He was trying to get my attention over all the other voices in my life. The rolling of the thunder was speaking louder than anything else, and I learned that if you can uncover the message, the breakthrough is around the corner. I was able to turn my wounds into wisdom.

One of the biggest forms of support came from friends. Just knowing others care about what you're going through can keep you in a positive state of mind. When Muhammad Ali was losing a fight, sometimes he would use the support of the ring's ropes to conserve a bit of energy. The ropes kept the fighter upright, and provided a quick breather to build just

## Personal, Professional, and Positive

enough energy for a knockout win. My friends were those ropes. You may have to be those ropes for someone someday. I know we don't feel strong all the time but are well equipped to outlast turbulent times.

Breakdowns can sometimes create breakthroughs. All of the greats have stories about trials and failures. God gives His hardest battles to His strongest soldiers. The mountains or giants in our lives love to call your name to remind you of all the times you've tried and failed. What would success be if you didn't experience setbacks? Stars can't shine without darkness. We have to be able to stand before that giant, even with only a slingshot and stones to regain rule over your life. You'll come out on the other side better than ever.

Rest in knowing that there is a solution to life's ups and down. Don't quit or throw in the towel, because this won't be the last storm you will have to face. The same boiling water that softens a potato hardens an egg. It's about what you're made of, not the circumstance. Life doesn't get easier as we grow older; you just get better at identifying and correcting your mistakes. Mistakes are proof that you're trying. Even if you strike out, keep going! Failure is a lesson, not a loss.

*Don't confuse your path with your destination. Just because it's stormy now doesn't mean that you aren't headed for sunshine.*

*– Unknown*

# Thirty

# Shine Like Nobody's Watching

***Challenge:*** *Make a Shine Jar. Write down on a piece of paper each good thing you did for someone else every day for one week, and put it in the jar.*

A GREAT MOTTO YOU'VE EVEN heard in this book is to dance like nobody's watching. I love this adage because when you stop focusing on what other people are thinking about you, then you can truly let loose and cut up on the dance floor. When you don't care about what others think of you, the weights come off and you can soar. Once you are self-confident, the thoughts of others no longer have power. When you are living your life in such a way that you are being good, doing good, and living well, do you really need a crowd to validate your wonderfulness? Would you still be amazing if no one saw you being amazing or living a gem-filled life? Of course you would.

A part of being truly happy is being content with oneself. Each of us should work on getting to the center of our purpose, passion, and joy. That's when you're filled to the brim from within and can spread love. Of course, making others happy is indeed a blessing to be able to give. But your life shouldn't rely solely on that. Start with impressing yourself and being happy with the gifts you have been given and are using. Don't live your life working hard to impress other people to get their approval.

*Personal, Professional, and Positive*

My definition of "shining" is this: shining is when it becomes about others and not about yourself.

> ☞ **Positive Hack**
> Once your Shine Jar is filled, do something nice for yourself!

When you shine like no one is watching, you are doing good for yourself and others, even if you don't receive the fanfare and pats on the shoulder. No longer do you feel compelled to tell others what good you've done. By your glowing nature and amazing personality, people will know that you are rooted and planted in helping others. It is no longer necessary to broadcast the favor you've bestowed on others.

The foundation of the "shine like nobody's watching" ideology is you feel good, do good, and live good. You do this each and every day, whether you have an audience of five thousand on Twitter and Facebook, or an audience of one. You aren't playing to the cameras and trying to put on a façade. You are able to be totally transparent because your actions are in tandem with your thoughts, and vice versa.

The reward for shining your brightest shouldn't come from accolades, mentions, follower counts, etc. Your reward may not be even something that you reap while on earth. The reward is actually in the deed itself and the way that you live your life. The feeling that you get when you were able to assist someone or make them smile is your reward. And that feeling is immeasurable and priceless.

When you shine like no one is watching, the person you are is the same person to everyone that comes across your path. If you had to ask twenty different people and they all would use some of the same positive adjectives to describe you, then chances are you are already operating in your spirit. This is the way to go through your life: as a person whose light shines wherever they go and to whomever they come across.

The world is such a dark place, so when you shine, it attracts people to you. It also offers a pathway that other people may not know existed. Before you know it, they are taking cues from you and are walking brightly as well, making the path clearer for others. And that darkness clouding our world begins to be drowned out by our shine. The brighter we shine, the better our planet will be.

In conclusion, your potential is limitless and so is your ability to light pathways. Begin to shine like nobody's watching and create a movement that is contagious. People will wonder what it is about you that is so magnetic, but you won't have to tell them. Your actions and deeds will prevail and so will your investment in doing good for others.

*Be the light shining in the darkness.*

*– Julie Reed*

# Dedication

We'd like to dedicate Personal, Professional, and Positive to the amazing memories of Michael A. Smith and Beulah Johnson. It is the life lessons gained from these people that provided the motivation to pursue, live and share the keys of excellence within this book, with readers as they pursue their passions.

# About the Authors

DANYELLE LITTLE, IS A MOM of two, professional blogger, owner of TheCubicleChick, author, and Digital Debutante. The CubicleChick.com was created to discuss topics important to working parents and entrepreneurs. Glamour Magazine, the Wall Street Journal, and Huffington Post Live have all tapped Danyelle to share her thoughts on newsworthy issues and trends.

TELIE WOODS, IS A PUBLISHER, author, entrepreneur and award wining sales leader who has generated millions for some of the country's top Fortune 500 organizations. With a Masters degree in Publishing, Mr. Woods co-founded online platform Think Positive Magazine. TPM is an authority in critical thinking; designed to empower, encourage and educate through quality content.

www.ingramcontent.com/pod-product-compliance
Lightning Source LLC
Chambersburg PA
CBHW060841050426
42453CB00008B/777